MA LARKIN'S

From
**THE
DARLING
BUDS OF MAY**

Perfick!

COOKING

• **Pearson Phillips and Jane Suthering** •

CHAPMANS

Chapmans Publishers Ltd
141-143 Drury Lane
London WC2B 5TB

First published by Chapmans 1991

ISBN 1-85592-568-0

Original television series based on the novels by H.E. Bates, Copyright © Evensford Productions Limited,
produced by Yorkshire Television Limited in association with Excelsior Group Productions Limited.
Executive Producers: Vernon Lawrence, Richard Bates and Philip Burley

Acknowledgements
The publishers and YOU Magazine would like to thank Pam Ferris

They also wish to thank Philip Dunn for taking YOU Magazine's photographs and Meg Jansz for assisting with the photography

Designed by Philip Mann/ACE Limited
Produced by Geoff Barlow
Origination by Studio One Origination Limited
Printed and bound in Great Britain by
Eagle Colourbooks Limited, Glasgow

CONTENTS

A BIT OF SAUCE

*B*it saucy, isn't it, me turning out a cookbook? Don't think I'd even read one before, let alone thought about writing one.

You can blame the General. He started it, one Sunday dinner time. What I like about the old poppet is the way he always comes out with a few buttery words before tucking in. 'The world would be a happier place,' he says, 'if everyone lived as well as this.'

Oh yes, I tell him. Want me to feed the rest of the world now as well as you lot? I wouldn't mind. Need a bigger kitchen, though.

Then up pipes Charlie, that's my son-in-law, the clever one, married to Mariette, my eldest. But you could write it all down, he says, so that other people could read about how you do it. Think of all the people having to cook for themselves now they can't get help. You could pass on some tips. Be good for the children, too.

The children? Blimey, the younger girls are talking about having flats in London, and something called a career. Don't know what use cooking's going to be for them. Anyway, anyone who thinks you can learn cooking from books needs their head testing. It's all technique, like something else I could name that you can't learn from books. Besides, I don't know no recipes, do I? Nothing that everyone doesn't know already. I just cook whatever is good at the time, whatever's in the garden or in the fridge. There's only one golden rule. *Make sure there's plenty of it.*

But the General won't let go. He's like a dog with a slipper. It's not what you cook, he says. It's how you cook it. It's how you make everyone round your table feel so, so . . . well, perfect. How do you make everything look so good and smell so good? How do you make this Yorkshire pudding come right, for instance?

Nothing much to that. You've just got to beat the living daylights out of the mixture, that's all, until you think it's lovely and smooth. Then you've got to have the oven good and hot, and watch no one opens the door half-way through. But putting it down on paper isn't going to help anyone get that right. There's another thing. About the only writing I've done since leaving school is the odd shopping list and the kid's names on the birth forms.

Then Charlie pipes up again. You could talk to me as you are doing it, he says. I could put it down, add some cooking times, oven temperatures, quantities, and we'd have a cookery book.

So that's what we've done, and a real how d'ye do it's been these past months, with him in the kitchen with his pen and his little book asking questions all the time and me having to explain everything I was doing. Still, we had some laughs, like the time he got me so confused I popped a raspberry mousse in the bottom of the oven to bake slowly for two hours and put a bowl of rice pudding in the fridge to set. We were rolling about the kitchen fit to bust when we found out. Didn't waste it, though. Served the mousse as hot raspberry syrup over ice cream. 'Ma's Surprise', Charlie called it. 'Surprise? It's a bloomin' miracle,' said Pop.

One of Charlie's questions had me stumped, though. He says I could start off by talking about how I learned to cook. Not in school, that's for sure. I was kneeling on a stool at the kitchen table knocking up jam tarts when I was four. And I can still remember my Dad finishing off the first apple pie I made. Gave me the taste for the whole cooking lark, that did. There's still nothing like seeing people eating up what you've cooked to make you feel wanted. Does something special for a girl, that. And it seems to go together with the other thing that makes a girl feel special. They say that if you get it right in the kitchen you'll find it'll go all right upstairs as well. Stands to reason. If a bloke doesn't like his grub he won't be much use for anything else. That's what I've found, anyway. So thank goodness my Mum showed me every-thing she knew.

fancy grill looks nice. So does the new, streamlined pop-up toaster – not that we ever use it. Doesn't make the toast thick enough.

It's my little empire, though, and it's a pleasure just to be there. Perhaps the mid-morning is the best. The kids have gone off to school, Pop's gone off to some deal, the babies are outside where I can see them. I've got rid of the breakfast and haven't started the dinner. The radio's playing that dah-di-dah-di, dah-di-dah-di progamme and I can have a cup of tea, look out of the window at the garden and the fields, with the chickens, the geese, the turkeys, the cow, the pigs, the vegetable patch, all the riches of the earth. And I can think about how I am going to bring it all in here and turn it into food that is going to make people happy and healthy.

Pop's fitted me out with one of these contemporary, all-electric, labour-saving kitchens, though I don't know whose labour it's supposed to be saving. I haven't noticed much difference. I knew where I was with the old range. I could bake any time with that, but the new electric cooker's got a mind of its own. And the cleaning! Still, the

So don't ask me how I learned cooking. It's one of those things that comes naturally. If you enjoy eating, then you enjoy cooking. And I'll tell you something else for nothing. You won't catch *me* sitting in London chasing after no career.

BREAKFAST

Of all the meals, I think breakfast is my favourite. It's like having a party to celebrate a new day and keep everybody's peckers up till dinner time. Nice and easy to cook, too.

I suppose you could say we have two breakfasts in our house. Pop usually has his tea and bread and cheese or porridge first thing before he goes off to do the pigs and the poultry. And the kids usually cut themselves a slice of something early, just to keep themselves going till breakfast proper.

But I like to have a lie-in until about half-past six. That gives me plenty of time to have everything sizzling by the time they all start coming in at half seven.

And they all want something different. One wants the bacon crisp and curly, another likes it soft and curly, another likes it soft and flat. Some like the big fat sausages, others the thin ones. Pop used to have an Irish landlady in London who gave him potato cake, so he has to have a couple of slabs of that every now and then to keep him happy.

I don't mind, as long as I know. I leave the eggs till last. Then they can say whether they want two or three.

It was just after we'd had breakfast the other morning that a young man from the Health Office or something came round with a leaflet. Wanted to know if we were eating properly. Not too bad, thank you, I tell him. But I was a bit worried about *him*. Didn't look much of an advertisement for no Health Office. 'Had your breakfast?' I asked him. Looking quite peaky. And he didn't look much better when I offered him what we'd just had – bacon, sausages, liver, mushrooms, fried bread and a couple of eggs. Went all pale and said did I realise I could be killing my family with breakfasts like that.

What? Strangling them with sausages?

No, he says. It's the polyester, or something. It's fat that blocks up the tubes and gives heart attacks. Well, that got me a bit riled up. So I told him a thing or two.

Pigs don't fly, I told him, and they don't kill people and give them heart attacks neither. God created pigs to eat, but he didn't create all the other things the poor souls living on top of each other in cities have to put up with, like not having good regular meals, trying to do things on an empty stomach, rushing about crammed together underground, never breathing proper air or seeing the sunlight, worrying about their taxes or their rates or all the other things they are always going on about on the telly. It's politicians and civil-servant snoopers like him that create all that and make life miserable and difficult for people. And then they have the cheek to come round lecturing us about what we should eat.

Bloomin' sauce!

Porridge

My grandma used to make porridge the evening before out of coarse oatmeal and put it in a box of hay overnight so it would be ready in the morning. And she still didn't always manage to get the lumps out.

Well, lumps in porridge can spoil your whole day. So we buy those packets with the picture of the cheerful old white-haired boy in the black hat on them. I do what he tells me on the packet, remembering specially to keep stirring, and in five minutes I've got better than anything grandma did, with never a lump in sight. Perfect, with cream and brown sugar on a cold dark winter morning. So that's that done.

Sausages

I get the bangers going first, because they take the longest. Big fat ones and medium-sized ones, with a few herbs and spices mixed in with the meat. Don't forget to prick 'em all over to stop them exploding. Fry them over a medium heat, turning them all the time so the skins get nice and brown all over. When they have browned up all the way round they'll be cooked through in the middle. Takes a good ten minutes.

What do I fry 'em in? A mixture of lard and butter, mostly. Lard stops them sticking and butter gives things a nice flavour. I make my own lard, of course – render it down from our own spare pig fat.

Bacon

If I haven't got any of my own bacon handy, I get cured middle back from the butcher. I get him to cut it so it's not too thick and not too thin. If it's too thick the fat doesn't go crispy. I get the scissors out to cut the rinds off. You're supposed to keep them for putting in soup, but we hardly ever eat soup at home. Pop says it's a waste of time and a way of filling you up so you won't want so much meat. So the cat gets them.

Pop likes his bacon to come out nice and flat, so I snip his with the scissors, every inch or so along the edge of the fat to stop it curling up. Some of the kids like it really curly, so I smooth theirs with the flat side of a knife before cooking it. Wavy as the Navy, it makes it.

Liver and Kidney

We always try and have a bit of 'kidney'. It's good for you. I always use lamb's kidney. Don't forget to cut 'em in half and snip out all the little white tubes. I usually dip them in a bit of flour before frying them in hot bacon fat. They just have to get nice and golden brown – the softer they are to the touch the pinker they'll be inside. So finish them as you like.

The liver needs frying towards the end. It can easily get tough if you cook it too long. We like it a bit pink inside, so we give it roughly the same treatment as the kidneys. Seems to go perfect with the bacon.

Potato Cake

You are supposed to use a hot, cast-iron griddle for this. I've got an old one, but I find I can do them quite nicely in one of my heavy frying-pans. I just mix up some left-over potato with a bit of milk and a pinch of salt. Add a drop of flour to bind it all together and roll it out on a floured board to about $1/2$-inch thick. Cut it into triangles and brown them up quickly on both sides in a bit of bacon fat.

The Rest

If there's mushrooms about in late summer, Pop or the kids will have brought some in. We usually fry up some tomatoes, too. Then there's the fried bread. Have to be quite careful with that. Pop says he likes it the way he likes his women – nicely browned on the outside and soft in the middle. So I cut quite thick slices and add a bit of my home-made dripping into the bacon fat, getting it smoky hot.

That just leaves the eggs. I fry them last in a coating of medium hot butter with a bit of lard added, so they don't splutter too much. Got to keep basting them with the fat, so the yolk and the top cook as well as the underneath. They all like 'em soft, so the yellow runs all over their fried bread.

You need a bit of variety to make life interesting. So occasionally I'll scramble the eggs. I put a drop of milk to each egg in the mixing bowl, as well as the salt and pepper, then add a dash of cream when they are beginning to firm up in the saucepan. Have to watch them, though. Keep them soft and on the runny side. Nothing worse than scrambled egg that's gone hard and dry, like that powder stuff they used to try and make us use in the war. If I've got some smoked salmon left over I'll cut that up and shove it in too.

If the fish van's been we'll sometimes forget all that and have a plate of kippers. I cook them in boiling water for a couple of minutes before bunging them under the grill with a knob of butter on them. Or sometimes we'll feel like a bit of smoked haddock, poached in milk very gently with blobs of butter for about 10 minutes.

Apart from all that it's just a matter of keeping the toast flowing and making sure there's plenty of what the egg said at breakfast time on the table ('ma-ma laid'). I make both lemon and orange. We can never make up our minds which we like best.

Lemon Marmalade

4-5lb of lemons
About 2 bags of sugar – 4lb

Scrub the lemons and cut them in half length-ways, then slice them as thin as you can. You have to pick out all the pips and keep them. We'll need them later.

Put the lemon slices in a large jam-pan with about ¾ pint of water. Tie up the lemon pips in a bit of muslin and bury them in the lemon slices. Cook it all over a very gentle heat for about 2 hours, then take out the bag of pips and squeeze out all the juice in the muslin back into the pan. Stir in the sugar and when it's all dissolved (not before!) turn up the heat a bit and cook for another hour or so until the mixture is ready to set. My test for this is to keep a saucer in the fridge, drop a little bit of the marmalade on it and put it back in the fridge for a moment. If the marmalade thickens on the saucer and you get a skin which wrinkles when you push your finger through it, then it's ready to be put in the jars. You shouldn't have any trouble with the lemon. It sets easy.

Pour it into your clean hot jars (I wash them and keep them in the oven until I want them). Lay waxed jam papers on top and leave to go cold before you fix the covers on with the elastic bands and do the labelling.

Orange Marmalade

This is a job for January or February, when you get those special little marmalade oranges from Spain. Sevilles, they call them.

3lb of oranges
Juice of two lemons
6 pints of water
About 3 bags of sugar – 6lb

Wash the oranges, cut them in half and squeeze out the juice into a pan. Then scrape out the pips and all the white pulpy stuff from each orange half and tie it all up in a muslin bag. Make sure you take all the pith out. It helps the marmalade to set. Cut all the peel into thin strips and put in the jam pan with the orange and lemon juice, the water and your muslin bag. Simmer it for about two hours until the strips of peel are nice and soft. By that time there ought to be only half as much liquid as you started with. Squeeze out the muslin bag and throw it away.

Stir in the sugar and let it melt over a really gentle heat – you'll get little bits of burnt sugar in the marmalade if you don't make sure it's all properly melted. Bring it to the boil and let it rip for about 15 minutes or so before testing it, using my old saucer method. If it isn't ready, boil it a bit longer and test again. It plays up sometimes but keep at it. Nothing worse than kicking off the day with runny marmalade.

Once it's ready, leave it alone to cool off for 15 minutes. That way all the peel will stay evenly mixed in the marmalade, and won't crowd up to one end of the jar. Then put it in the hot jars, top it off with waxed discs and cover when it's cold.

Under the Tree

I don't know what it is about eating outdoors. But the food tastes better. And everybody seems to switch into a party mood as soon as we sit down at our wooden table under our lovely big tree. I'd do it every day if our climate was up to it.

It's like having a picnic, except we have proper meals with all the trimmings – big Sunday lunches, with the family and a few friends sitting on the mixture of chairs and benches we've collected over the years. We have a separate table for the drinks, good white tablecloth, best china.

Charlie's got an Italian name for it, Al Fresco, though I don't know who he was when he was at home. He says the Italians eat like that all the time, and that's why they are so cheerful and full of laughter.

Well, I don't know about that. There's something else they are dab hands at, so I hear. And I reckon eating out of doors helps that along, too. It's being in the middle of all that nature, I suppose.

Roast Pheasant with Chipolatas and Trimmings

We're never short of pheasants in the season, as you know. I put a lot in the freezer so we can have them all the year round. They need a couple of days in the fridge to thaw out slowly. I can pluck, draw and truss 'em in my sleep by now. But we don't like them too gamey. Some people hang them for a couple of weeks or more, depending on the weather. But that's not for us. We can get quite enough flavour and tenderness without having them high as a parson's hat.

I use one bird for every two people and then add another brace for seconds or to eat cold.

Wipe them inside and out with a damp cloth, then sprinkle them with salt, pepper and a bit of chopped thyme. Melt a good dollop of butter (4oz) in a roasting-tin and brown the birds on all sides until they're golden, but don't let the butter burn whatever you do.

Then I put them in a fairly hot oven, about 400°F/ 200°C/gas mark 6. I keep the breast moist the same way I do with other birds, starting with 15 minutes or so lying on each breast so that the leg juices come down naturally. Then I turn them over right way up and cook for another half an hour, basting them a lot. I often add more butter so there's plenty to baste with, and a glass or two of left-over red wine as well. That way you get some nice juices that bubble down into a thin gravy and you don't need to do anything else to it.

Of course, it's all the trimmings that are the making of a dish of pheasants – a spot of watercress if you can get it, and lots of little chipolata sausages. I put them in a tin in the oven for about half an hour or so until they are golden all over. They don't really need any extra fat, but they do need turning over now and again.

They always want their 'game chips'. Well, I have been known to make wafer-thin potato slices, dry them in a tea-towel and deep-fry them in hot fat. But normally I get lots of bags of crisps and nobody but me knows.

Bread sauce is another favourite, and that's easy. Just pop a couple of pints of milk in a saucepan with a couple of peeled onions, two bay leaves and 3 or 4 cloves. Bring it just to the boil, then leave it alone for 15 minutes or so while you're getting on with something else, like peeling the sprouts. When you are ready add about 6 heaped tablespoons of fresh bread-crumbs – about 6oz – and a good dollop of butter – 2oz – and cook it over the lowest possible heat until it's thickened a bit to a nice sauce. Then you've got to remember to take out the onion, bay leaves and cloves – count 'em – and add salt and pepper until you think it's right.

I like plenty of mashed potatoes, whipped up with a good splash of cream, to go with pheasant. It's good for soaking up the gravy. Then you need something green in the way of a vegetable. Brussels sprouts are my favourite, and they are just coming in when we get the pheasants fresh in the Autumn. Even when they are new from the garden, hardly needing any peeling, I nick a little cross with a knife in the bottom so they cook nice and even. They'll go soggy and spoil if you have to leave them in too long to soften up the bottoms. I love the small tight ones you get after the first frost. Nothing like a bit of frost to tighten up your Brussels!

Roast Leg of Pork with Brown Onions, Stuffing and Apple Sauce

The fillet end of one of our legs of pork weighs about 8lb. That's fine for us, but we're a big family. You could always buy a smaller piece. It just needs wiping over. But if you want good crackling you'll have to take a bit of trouble scoring lines close together in the rind, with the sharpest knife you've got. Then rub it with a little oil or melted lard and sprinkle it with salt.

I cook it in a hottish oven – about 375°F/ 190°C/gas mark 5 – for as long as it needs, which can be as much as four hours for one of our big pieces. You must never let it be under-cooked like beef or lamb, so that it comes out pink inside. The only way to test it is to stick a fork or skewer through the middle and make sure that the juices come out clear and not in the slightest bit pink. It'll take half an hour per pound, at least.

To cook the onions round the joint I just peel them and add them a good halfway through the cooking time. I like to keep the onions whole, so I pick medium-sized ones, skin them and just turn them in the pan juices, adding about a pint of stock or water. That extra liquid will help to keep the meat moist as well. But a warning! You can't baste the joint after you've put the liquid in the pan, or else you'll make the crackling soggy.

I love sage and onion stuffing, and that's another easy job. Chop up 4 medium onions and fry them in a lump of butter – about 2oz – until they're soft. Stir in about 4 heaped serving-spoons of fresh bread-crumbs – about 4oz – and about 3 table-spoons of chopped fresh sage. Mix it all together, moisten it with some stock and add salt and pepper. Then put it in a baking-dish and pop it in the oven with the roast for the last hour or so of the cooking. You can stir it up from time to time and I usually take a few spoonfuls of the meat juices and stir those in as well.

Apple sauce – mustn't forget that. It's just lots of apples, peeled, cored and chopped. Then cook them in a pan with a little sugar to taste. At the end, when it's cooked to a pulp, beat in a good dollop of butter.

Roast Goose

Our geese end up weighing about 10lb, which should be enough for 6-8 people. So I cook a couple at a time for our family, and three to be on the safe side if we've got guests.

I make the same sage and onion stuffing that I serve with pork, stuffing some in the geese and cooking any that's left separately in the oven. I fill the neck end with the stuffing, wrapping the flap of skin under the bird and holding it tight with skewers. You've got to be a bit careful with the skin of a goose if you want it nice and crispy. After I've wiped the bird, I rub some flour into the skin all over, with a bit of of salt and pepper. Then I prick the skin all over, with a fork, so that the fat will get out. I do my usual trick to keep the breast moist, starting the bird upside down, although come to think of it that's the right way up when it's alive . . . anyway breast down.

I start with a hot oven – about 425°F/220°C/gas mark 7 – for the first half hour or so. Then I turn it down to medium, add a splash of water to the roasting tin and cook it for about 1½ hours at 350-375°F/180-190°C/gas mark 4-5.

It's time then to turn the bird over, breast up, and give it another 1½ to 2 hours, until it's cooked through. Like all the other birds, the best way to tell is with a skewer in the thickest part of the leg to see if the juice runs clear. You can leave it to rest for a while on a big plate while you make the gravy. Pour off most of the fat from the roasting tin, then stir in a good spoonful of plain flour and cook till it's golden. Then add a drop of wine and enough stock to make a nice thin gravy. When you've got it tasting right, with a drop of salt and pepper, you can leave it simmering until you are ready to serve everything up.

Asparagus goes well with it, and so do new green peas. I sit down to pod them with a glass of something while the goose is cooking, then boil them fast at the last moment with a bit of sugar and a sprig of mint. Toss them in butter after you've drained them. The best potatoes you'll ever taste are those roasted in goose fat.

Roast Guinea Fowl

They eat a treat during the summer, but you've got to watch out for the meat drying out and losing all its flavour. There's not a lot on them, though. One of them only feeds two people, and I usually bung in an extra couple for luck. A sprig or two of parsley and tarragon inside each one with a knob of butter helps keep the flavour.

After you've given them a wipe over with a damp cloth and put them in the roasting tin cover them with plenty of melted butter and some rashers of streaky bacon or pork fat.

Cook them in a medium hot oven – 350°F/180°C/gas mark 4 – for about an hour, basting them a lot so they stay moist. Then I take the bacon off and let the birds get golden brown for a last 20 minutes or so. While the birds are browning is a useful time to get the green vegetables going.

Make some gravy in the usual way, pouring off the fat from the pan and add a sprinkling of plain flour. Stir it well on top of the stove and add a good splash of wine or sherry and plenty of stock. I use about a pint of liquid in all. Simmer it for a few minutes, adding salt and pepper to taste.

Steak and Kidney Pie

When I'm making my steak and kidney pie I ask the butcher for a few nice thick slices of stewing steak and a dozen or so lamb's kidneys. Ox and pig's kidneys are just a bit too strong for this to my thinking and spoil the flavour of the pie.

If you're making a small pie, you'll need about a quarter of this lot. This'll make one great big pie and a baby one as well.

About 6lb of stewing steak
A dozen or so lamb's kidneys – around 2lb
3-4 heaped serving-spoons of plain flour – about 4oz
Plenty of salt and pepper
2 good dollops of beef dripping – about 4oz

2 large onions – about 1lb
A couple of pints of brown stock
Puff pastry to cover the pies

the middle of my pies sometimes, specially a big one. That's just to hold the pastry up. It can sometimes fall in if you're not careful, or if the oven's playing up. Warm up the extra gravy, it'll be good on the potatoes.

Roll out the pastry and put a roof on the pie. I put a band of pastry round the rim of the dish first, sticking it to the edge of the dish with water. That gives the top something to hold on to. Then I put the rolled-out pastry on top, sticking that down on the band round the rim with water and pressing it down really well. I usually crimp the edge into a pattern with a knife – 'knocking up' we used to call it. Then I make a couple of slashes in the top to let the steam out and brush it all with beaten egg to give it a nice shiny finish. A work of art, a nice pie.

Bake in a hot oven – about 425°F/220°C/ gas mark 7 – until the pastry is good and brown, about half an hour. Then turn it down about 50-75°F and cook for another 20-30 minutes until the meat is hot all through.

My Trifle

The main thing you've got to know about with a trifle is the custard. There are no set rules for the rest, you just dollop in what you've got in the way of sponge cake and fruit – sliced up bananas, peaches, berries, whatever you fancy.

Make the custard first. While that's cooking and cooling you can throw everything else together.

Cut all the meat into cubes and take all the white gubbins out of the middle of the kidneys (I chop them a bit smaller than the steak). Then toss it all in flour with loads of salt and pepper as well.

You'll need a big pan for this. Fry the chopped onions in the dripping until they are soft and golden, and add the meat. You can brown it, if you've got time, but I don't always go that far. Add the stock (bit of left-over red wine doesn't do no harm, either) and bring it to the boil. Then cook it really slow for a couple of hours until it's nice and tender. I usually do this the day before I need the pie, because – just like a stew – it seems to taste better the next day.

I add lots of chopped parsley to the meat and put it in my pie dishes. Keep some of the gravy back so the pastry doesn't get too soggy – about half full should do. I put an old cup in

For mine I use:
Plain cake sandwiched with raspberry or strawberry jam, cut up into small bits, enough to half fill my trifle bowl – about 12oz
About 1/4 to 1/3 of a bottle of medium dry sherry (7fl oz)
A good sprinkling of crushed macaroon biscuits – 4oz

For the custard you'll need:
2 pints of milk
A split vanilla pod or a couple of bay leaves
4 eggs plus 4 yolks
2 heaped serving-spoons of sugar – 2oz
Plenty of whipped cream for the top

Start of by putting the cake in the trifle bowl, pouring the sherry over it and sprinkling it with the macaroon biscuits. Add some fruit if you want to. Heat the milk (don't boil it!) with the vanilla or bay leaf and leave for a while so the flavour gets into the milk. Beat the eggs and sugar in a big bowl and pour the warm milk in, stirring it up. Cook it over a pan of simmering water. But keep an eye on it all the time, it mustn't get too hot or else the eggs will curdle. Keep on stirring with your wooden spoon until you can feel it thickening so it coats the back of the spoon when you hold it up.

Once it's cooled a bit, pour it through a sieve on to the sponge cake. Then pop it in the fridge. When it's cold top it with lots of whipped cream and anything else you fancy, like toasted almonds or glacé cherries. At Christmas I put on candied fruit and those crystallised violets.

15

MA'S SPECIALS

Pop always gives a young sow a bottle of stout before she starts feedin' her litter. It settles her down, he says. Same with me. Before getting on with one of our big family do's I like a couple of minutes settling meself down with a glass of Guinness. There's far to much rushing about fretting and worrying in this world, specially in kitchens. I know some women who spend hours trying something a bit classy and elaborate. And then they get all upset when it doesn't come out right.

Well, I've got plenty to do around here, what with the butter and the hens and the garden and the babies and all. I haven't got all day to sweat over a stove. And I've noticed that if there is any fretting going on, it seems to get the cow on edge. She doesn't milk right. So what I prefer is to stick to the things I could do in my sleep. Ma's Specials, Pop calls 'em. Then it all runs like clockwork, sweet as a nut. Cooks itself, almost.

Roast Leg of Lamb, Braised Potatoes, Mint Sauce, Marrow Baked with Cheese

I get the butcher to choose me a couple of legs of British lamb that have a good, even covering of fat on them. Can't think why some people complain about having fat on their joints. You need that to keep the meat moist, and even then you'll need to keep basting it. Nothing worse than dried up meat.

I like to cook it in a medium hot oven, that's about 350°F/180°C/gas mark 4, so it doesn't shrink too much. You can always turn the oven up for a bit of a blast towards the end if you don't think the fat's crisping up enough.

I start off by giving the meat a wipe over with a damp cloth – you never know quite where it's been if you haven't reared it yourself. Then I just pop it in my big roasting-tin, which is big enough for two legs and plenty of potatoes round them besides. Shake some salt and pepper over them, and a good dollop of beef dripping if the meat looks a bit lean.

The oven should have been warming up. I put the joints in round about half-past ten in the morning for dinner time. They usually take about 2½ hours. Some people will tell you they should stay in for about half an hour per pound of weight. Trouble is, meat's all different. I suppose I've been at this lark for so long, I can tell when a joint should go in just by looking at it. What you're aiming for is meat that's nice and crispy on the outside and moist and tender in the middle. Of course, before dishing up I slice myself a little bit off the end to make sure, but you can stick a skewer or a fork in the thickest part to check the colour of the juices. The more done the meat is the clearer they will be.

I always put potatoes round the lamb. They soak up the juices lovely. I peel a couple for everyone at the table, plus a few over for luck. There aren't usually any left over, but if there are you can slice them up and have them fried with cold meat for supper. I put the potatoes in after the lamb has had about an hour, so that there's some hot fat already in the tin. Cut them up quite chunky, toss them around in the fat to coat them and then turn them over when you're basting the meat. They come out a sort of crispy, soggy roast.

I usually have five or six other veg on the table, everyone has their favourites. One of mine is marrow, done with a cheese sauce – I peel and slice it, cutting out the seeds because they make it a bit watery if you don't watch out. I steam or boil the chunks of marrow until they are tender, then cover them in my own rich cheese sauce, which I make like this:

For every pint of milk I use:

One big marrow
A good lump of butter – 2oz
About 1½ serving-spoons of plain flour – 2oz
A good pinch of dry mustard
A handful of grated Cheddar – about 4oz
Salt and Pepper

Melt the butter in a saucepan and stir in the flour and mustard, keeping it moving with a wooden spoon over a gentle heat until

Cooked Ham with New Potatoes Richly Buttered and Freckled with Parsley

The main thing is finding a pan large enough to cook the piece of ham in. A whole boned gammon can be pretty big. Lovely thing to cut at, though. And it's so easy. All you have to do is stick it in the pan and simmer it till it's nice and tender. The best thing to do would be to measure your largest pan and get the butcher to cut a piece to fit it.

Cover it with cold water and bring it to the boil very slowly. Then pour off the water. It gets rid of some of the saltiness. Then cover it with cold water and start again. (No, of course you don't put any salt in the water. Blimey, use your loaf!) Bring it to a gentle simmer and just leave it blooping quietly until it's tender, according to its size. I know that a piece for my big pan put on after breakfast takes until midday. It weighs around 8lb, and if it cooks between 8.30 in the morning and 12 o'clock, that's $3^1/_2$ hours. Work it out according – 25 minutes per pound, plus a bit over for luck.

Leave it to cool in the water a bit. Then take it out and peel off the skin as soon as you can handle it.

There's nothing else to it, apart from the vegetables. I love new potatoes in their skins straight from the ground – washed, of course! Don't overcook them so that they fall apart. The little ones only take about 12 or 15 minutes. A sprig of mint in the water makes them nice. Then when they are done toss them in lots of chopped parsley, fresh from the garden.

Young broad beans go well with it, too. They are good just covered in butter, provided they are young and tender. But for a change I sometimes do 'em an old Kent way – covered in fresh cream that's been thickened with egg yolks and flavoured with chopped tarragon. You warm up the sauce, of course, but watch out you don't let the cream boil or the eggs will curdle. Hope you've got some helping hands for the bean shelling, because you need a load of pods for a family like ours. We're lucky if we get 4 ounces of beans out of a pound of pods some days.

it's lightly golden. Stir in the milk and keep cooking while you feel it thicken. When it's quite thick, stir in the cheese and add as much salt and pepper as you think it needs.

Pour this over the cooked marrow in a big oven-proof dish and top it up with some more grated cheese, if you fancy it. Leave it in the bottom of the oven for a good three-quarters of an hour, just as the lamb is coming to the end of its cooking time.

Oh, don't forget the mint sauce. I've got a tip for chopping the mint leaves – they seem to chop easier if you sprinkle sugar on them. Then I put them in a bowl with a couple of tablespoons of boiling water and the same of vinegar and leave it to stand for a while.

Venison

Pop gets hold of a haunch or a loin from time to time, and the first thing we do is skin it and hang it up in one of the outhouses for two or three weeks. It's nice and cool and airy out there. Watch out for flies and that. I've got one of those big old meat-safes made of fine wire mesh, which is perfect for the job. If it's young meat it'll probably be tender enough to cook straight away after that. But if it's a bit older I like to give it a couple of days soaking in a mixture of vegetables and some of the red wine Pop calls his cooking wine. It can be very dry, venison. No fat on it worth talking about.

For the soaking mixture I chop up a large onion, a carrot, and a couple of sticks of celery and put them in a bowl with a bunch of herbs and some pepper. I lay the venison on top of that, then cover it all with a bottle of red wine and leave it somewhere cool, turning the meat now and again. It gives it quite a strong flavour when it's cooked, but it does make it nice and moist and tender.

I cut the loin or leg fillet up into good slices, without any bone. 'Escalopes,' Charlie calls them. Then I give them a good bash with the rolling-pin to flatten them and make them a bit more tender.

Then I sprinkle them with salt and pepper, and fry them slowly in a pan that is swimming in butter, more the better. I usually give them five minutes a side. Then I serve them up with some of the buttery juices, plenty of my redcurrant jelly and a good choice of vegetables.

Wild Duck with Orange Sauce

Pop usually brings in mallard, which is the largest wild duck. But sometimes we get a few widgeon or teal. There's not much on them, about enough for two from the bigger birds. But with a teal you really need one each.

We hang 'em in the cool for a week or a bit more, depending on the weather, keeping an eye open for flies. Don't care for them too high, just until I can pluck them easily. I always sort out the giblets from the rest of the stuff when drawing our birds. They make good stock.

For a brace of mallard you'll need:

A good dollop of butter, about 2oz
About 1/2 pint of nice, rich stock
2 oranges
A dash of port
A level serving-spoon of flour, about 1/2 oz
Salt and pepper

I like to brown the birds first, so I fry them in butter until they're golden all over. Then I pour in the stock and sprinkle them with the grated rind of an orange and plenty of salt and pepper.

I usually put them in a deepish dish (the big one from my new Pyrex casserole set does nicely). The lid keeps them moist while they are in the oven, as they get a bit dry sometimes. So do I, round about this stage.

19

I cook them in a hot oven, about 400°F/200°C/gas mark 6, for 30–40 minutes. They don't take anywhere near as long as a domestic duck.

Take them out of the casserole and keep them warm while you make the sauce. Pour the duck juices into a pan and whisk in a bit of flour. Cook it over a medium heat, stirring it while it thickens up. I add in the juice of the oranges and a drop of port or any left-over red wine and then let it bubble a bit into a rich, tempting sauce. You have to taste it, of course. It may need some salt or pepper. A little bit of lemon juice brings out the flavour, too. I dress 'em up a bit to serve them, with orange slices round the side of the plate and a bit of watercress. The better it looks, the better it eats. I put the sauce in a jug so people can help themselves.

Trout Swimming in Brown Butter

Better not ask where he gets 'em. But they are always nice and fresh. So you won't really need much more than the trout and some butter for this.

Clean and dry as many trout as you want to cook, then dip them in plain flour which has been seasoned with salt and pepper. Melt a good knob of butter (about an ounce for every

fish) in a frying pan. Then pop the fish in and fry them until they are crisp and golden on both sides. You'll soon learn how long to give them, but you can tell if they are done by pressing them with your finger and finding out if they feel firm. Or you can slip a little knife into the fish down to the bone. The flesh changes colour when it's cooked, getting paler and not so wet-looking.

Take out the trout when they're done, keep them in a dish and add another dollop of butter to the pan. Cook that until it's a nice golden liquid, then squeeze in as much lemon juice as you like and pour it over the fish. Serve 'em with a couple of wedges of lemon and some parsley.

Easy as a church gate and you won't find no more perfect way with trout.

Beef Stew with Orange and Prunes

With stew the longer and slower you cook it, the tastier it will be. And it always seems better when you have a second go at it. So I make big lots so that there is enough to come again. You can stew almost anything, but my special and everyone's favourite is beef with prunes and a hint of orange to it. The fruit lightens and sweetens the meat.

A big lump of stewing beef – 4lb
  A large lump of butter – 3oz
  A drop of oil to heat up with the butter – 1 tablespoon
  2 medium onions – peeled and chopped
  Some bacon – 4 rashers off the back, finely chopped up
  About 2 heaped serving-spoons of plain flour – 2oz
  Beef stock – 2 pints or more
  The rind of 2 oranges, chopped up
  The juice of 4 oranges
  Some prunes – about 10oz
  Lots of chopped parsley
  Salt and pepper
  A drop of vinegar – I use a couple of teaspoons

I've got a big casserole for stews that will go on top of the stove and in the oven.

Trim up the meat, getting rid of some of the fat and any gristly bits. Then cut it into medium-sized pieces – they'll be about an inch or more square, I suppose. Heat up the butter and the oil in the casserole and brown the meat quickly all round. You will probably need to do it in several goes. Take the meat out when it's browned. I put it to one side on the upturned lid of the casserole. Then put the onion and the bacon into the buttery meaty juices that are left in the pan and let them cook slowly until the onion has started to turn gold.

Put in the flour, stir it round to coat the onion and bacon and let it cook for a minute or two, but don't let it catch. Then stir in the stock, the orange rind and the juice, the prunes, a good dollop of the parsley and the meat. Season it with a bit of salt and pepper and bring it to the boil.

Then put the lid on the casserole and move it into the oven. If you are in a hurry you could give it 2 hours at a low heat – 325°F/170°C/gas mark 3. Better still would be 3 hours, lower still. The meat has to be tender. Jab it with a fork to see how its getting on.

Whatever you do, you need to give a final blast on top of the stove with the lid off, to give the juice a bit of extra body. So, take it out of the oven, give it a stir, add the drop of vinegar and cook it uncovered for about 15 minutes, with the occasional stir to make sure it isn't catching at the bottom. Taste it to see if it needs anything, sprinkle more parsley on top and serve.

It goes well with boiled potatoes and lovely winter roots like parsnips and carrots.

Cheese Pudding

I read in a magazine that this is the Bishop of Dover's favourite supper. So I'll know what to give him if he calls round.

1 pint of milk
A lump of butter, about 2oz
4 eggs
2 good handfuls of grated cheese, about 8oz. You want a good strong cheese, like a lump of that mature Cheddar or Red Leicester
About 2 teacups of breadcrumbs – about 4oz only don't squash them in when you are measuring them or else the pudding will be heavier than it ought to be
Salt, pepper and mustard powder

If there's a drop of wine or beer handy, I soak the breadcrumbs in that. But that means you cut down on the milk or it'll be too runny.

Warm the milk and the butter until the butter is all melted. Then pour it on to the beaten eggs. Add everything else and plenty of salt and pepper. About half a teaspoon of the dry mustard should pep it up a bit. A drop of Worcester helps, too.

It's best if you leave the mixture for half an hour or so to soak in the breadcrumbs. Then pour it all into an oven dish and bake it in a medium hot oven – about 375°F/ 190°C/gas mark 5 – for about 45 minutes. You can tell if it is done. It'll be all puffy and golden brown, but just a bit wobbly when you shake it. All right, wait for it. . .

'Just like you, Ma. . .'
Thank you. Not complaining, though, are you?

Rice Pudding

A great old standby, which needs practically no time to prepare and can be stuck in the oven to look after itself. But I need a big one for all my lot. Unless you've got a family like ours, who all want a bit of the browned-up skin, you could cut the quantities by half. I use:
3-4 serving-spoons of pudding rice – 4oz
A knob of butter – 1oz
3 pints of milk
A pinch of salt
2 serving-spoons of sugar – 2oz

Rinse the rice in a sieve than put it in a big ovenproof dish with all the rest of the ingredients and stir it up. Sprinkle the top with nutmeg and pop it in the oven for a good couple of hours or so on a low heat – 300-325°F/ 150-170°C/gas mark 2-3.

You just have to give it a stir after about an hour, then leave it until the rice is soft and the milk has made that lovely brown skin on the top.

I usually serve it with a jug of fresh cream.

THE STRAWBERRY LARK

You'd think we'd get tired of strawberries, spending whole days pickin 'em. 'Course you do, if you pick and eat all the time. But we don't do that. A few, maybe. Some of the first big king jobs at the end of the stalks, all warm from the sun, firm and fresh. But best of all is to wait until we bring a basket home and sit down to a bowl of them, with sugar and our Jersey cream on top. We mash the sugar and the cream and the pink juice all up together. It's like eating summertime. That's what I think of as strawberries.

We grow a few of our own – Royal Sovereigns, nice fat red ones, though you've got to watch for mould. For a bit later we've got Fillbasket. Good name for them, too. Fill a basket in no time with those. For a special early taste we leave jam jars down the rows and put some of the bunches of fruit in 'em, so they're ready as Freddy in no time.

We've got raspberries as well, of course. Good for courtin', raspberry picking. Never short of raspberries all summer as long as Primrose has got some young man she's decided she's in love with.

I usually leave the strawberry jam-making till a bit late in the season, round about middle to late August. You can use the little round ones that comes late for that. And don't let 'em be too ripe. They set better when they're a bit on the under-ripe side. I have a job setting the strawberry jam as it is, not like the gooseberries or the blackcurrants. I don't get it right sometimes. 'Hello,' says Pop. 'It's one of Ma's runny years.' So now I bung in plenty of lemon to be on the safe side.

By the way, make sure you've got a nice big saucepan or preserving pan for jam-making, because it has to boil fast and you don't want it running over. Mine's a nice wide, heavy one that brings the steam off good and quick. It all helps with the setting.

Strawberry Jam

About 8 of those ½ lb punnets of strawberries
Juice of 3 lemons
Not quite 2 bags of white sugar – about 3½ lb

Hull the strawberries – a nice sitting down job, this. Then stew them with the lemon juice until they are really soft, for about half an hour over a gentle heat.

Stir in the sugar. I've got a special, long-handled wooden spoon for that. When you've got all the sugar dissolved into the liquid, bring it to the boil and let it rip at a fast boil for about 15 minutes, or until the jam is ready to set. You'll remember the trick for seeing if it's ready – put a bit on a cold saucer, let it cool down and then push it with your finger. If the skin wrinkles, it's done. If not, give it a bit longer.

You have to let it cool for a while in the pan before putting it in the jars. Otherwise it will be too liquid and all the fruit will float to the top.

Don't forget to have the jars clean and hot. I put mine in the oven for a bit. Then cover the filled pots with those special waxed jam covers. We put sticky labels on with the name of the jam and the date – another nice job for the kids.

Raspberry Jam

About 4lb of raspberries
2 tablespoons of lemon juice
2 bags of white sugar – 4lb

Make it the same way as the strawberry jam.

Strawberry Mousse Ice Cream

It doesn't matter if the strawberries are a bit mushy for this. You're going to have to squash them anyway.

About 4 of those ½ lb punnets of strawberries
About 4 serving-spoons of sugar – 4oz
Juice of a lemon – that helps bring out the flavour
4 egg whites (if you're making custard you'll have some egg whites left over)
Pinch of salt – something else to bring out the flavour
1 pint of fresh thick cream

Crush the strawberries. You can do this by pressing them all through a sieve, which gets rid of a lot of the seeds at the same time. Add some of the sugar while you're crushing them. That makes it a lot easier. And stir in the lemon juice.

Whisk the egg whites until they're stiff, with a pinch of salt, just like you're starting off meringues. Then whisk in the rest of the sugar. Whip up the cream with a whisk until its floppy thick. Not too much, though – don't want to turn it into butter. Then stir everything together.

Pour it into a nice big bowl and pop it in the deep-freezer until it's hardened up proper. It'll be ready for tea if you get it made in the morning.

Maids of Honour

This is where a lot of raspberry jam ends up. Maids of Honour are one of Pop's favourites. Could be something to do with the brandy I slosh in 'em.

You'll have to make up some curds the day before for this. I've usually got some on the go in the little pantry I call my dairy, using milk left over after I've skimmed the cream off for the butter.

To get curds for the tarts you'll need:
2 pints of milk
2 heaped serving-spoons of sugar – 2oz
4 teaspoons of that bottled rennet

Warm up the milk and the sugar – not too hot, just warm. Stir in the rennet and leave it for half an hour or so until it starts to set like junket. Line a sieve with muslin, pop the mixture in and let it drain overnight. Or you can hang your muslin bags from hooks over a bowl if you like.

You'll also need:
2 more heaped serving-spoons of sugar – 2oz
3 good dollops of butter – about 3oz
2 eggs
2 heaped serving-spoons of ground almonds – 2oz
A couple of tablespoons of brandy
Enough puff pastry to line about 30 little bun tins –
about 12oz (you'll have to read my chapter about baking if you want to know how I set about making that). I roll it out nice and thin.
Raspberry jam

Beat up the butter, the sugar and the curds. Then beat in the eggs, the ground almonds and the brandy.

Roll out the pastry, nice and thin, and put it in your little bun tins. Then go round putting a blob of the raspberry jam in the bottom of each one. Go round again, spreading a blob of the curd mixture on top. Make sure you spread it right to the edge of the pastry, otherwise the jam will come bubbling up the sides and make a mess of everything.

Bake them in a hot oven. The puff pastry needs about 425°F/220°C/gas mark 7 until they are nice and golden – it'll be about 25 minutes. They rise lovely, but then they curtsy down when they come out of the oven.

Raspberry Tart

This always reminds me of that religious bit that comes on the radio over breakfast, Lift Up Your Hearts. For us it is always the sign it's time for the kids to be leaving for school. 'Come on,' Pop says. 'Raspberry Tarts time.' That's why when we have raspberry tart on the table the twins always sing out, 'Lift up your hearts . . .'

I usually hunt in the cocktail cabinet for a drop of kirsch to pour into the eggy custard that goes on to this tart. Helps lift up your hearts a bit more, that does. You also need:
Enough shortcrust pastry to line a large pie dish. I use a big 10-inch dish that needs around ¾lb of pastry
Enough raspberries to fill half the dish – about 1lb
3 eggs
½ pint of fresh thick cream
About two-thirds of a cup of caster sugar – about 4oz
1 tablespoon arrowroot or cornflour

Roll out the pastry and line the big pie dish. Don't forget to press the edges down well, like I say later in my bit about baking. Then I line it with a sheet of greaseproof and weigh it down by filling it with some of the old dried beans that I keep in a jar, specially for baking pastry cases.

It'll need about 20 minutes in a hot oven, starting off at around 400°F/200°C/gas mark 6. But after about 10 minutes the edges of the pastry will have begun to cook all right, so you can take the paper and the beans out and let the bottom dry out.

Leave it to cool for a while, then put the raspberries in the bottom. Beat everything else together into a custard and pour it over the top of the fruit. Put it back into the oven (350°F/180°C/gas mark 4) until the custard is all golden and set, which can take about an hour. It shouldn't wobble if you shake it.

We like it best when it's still warm. And I usually sprinkle a bit of extra sugar on top for luck.

4 heaped serving-spoons of icing sugar – 4oz
1 pint of fresh thick cream
4 egg whites

Easy as pie, just wash and hull the strawberries then crush them with the sugar. I sometimes add a dash of orange liqueur as well.

Whip the cream until it's thick and whisk the egg whites with a pinch of salt until they're stiff. Then fold the cream and the egg whites into the strawberry mixture.

I just pile it into dishes and keep it nice and fresh in the fridge until we want it.

Raspberry Mousse

Same technique as for strawberries.

Mixed Fruit Pie

I use my medium pie-dish for this. I suppose it takes 2-3lb of fruit. I like to use a mixture of raspberries and/or strawberries with some apple. Even banana mixes in well.

Prepare all the fruit – that means peeling, coring and slicing the apples, peeling and slicing the bananas, hulling the berries and cutting the strawberries in half if they are big ones.

Layer them up in the pie dish with a sprinkling of sugar between each layer. If you are using things like gooseberries you may need a bit more sugar – but you can always add it when it's on your plate. Always make sure the dish is full of fruit and piled up in a mound, because it shrinks a lot when it cooks.

Then I top it with shortcrust pastry – it takes about ¾lb, I suppose. I've got a bit of a trick to stop the roof falling in during the cooking: make a long strip of pastry and damp it down well to stick on the edge of the pie-dish, then when you're putting on the rolled-out bit of pastry for the top you've got a good foundation to stick it on. It doesn't always work, but even if the roof does collapse, I wouldn't lose any sleep over it. It all goes down the same way!

Freezing Strawberries

In a good summer we'll have strawberries from May right through to October. And plenty of raspberries as well. But I still miss them in the winter time, specially for cooking. So since we got the deep-freezer I have had a go at freezing them.

All you do is lay the berries out on a tray so that they're not on top of each other and freeze them until they're solid. Then you just load them into bags, or one of those plastic boxes, and you can have strawberry mousse all the year round.

Strawberry Mousse

To make enough for six:
About 3 of the ½lb punnets of strawberries

Trim it up nicely at the edges, pinching it into a pattern with your fingers if you like. Then make a couple of slashes in the top to let the steam out. Brush the pastry with milk or egg white and sprinkle it with plenty of sugar.

It needs quite a hot oven – about 425°F/220°C/gas mark 7 to start with – for 15 minutes or so to get the pastry going.

Then down to medium heat – about 350°F/180°C/gas mark 4 – for another three-quarters of an hour or more. The fruit should feel tender if you stick a skewer in, and the pastry should be golden.

Serve it with lots of fresh cream, and a sprinkling of more sugar if you want it.

DROP IN FOR TEA

I reckon there aren't many things that'll get the juices going like the smell of fresh baking that comes from my kitchen most afternoons around teatime. It certainly gets old Pop going. He's in from the yard sharp at four, looking for his afternoon nibble.

Funny thing is, that old baking smell seems to drift round the whole neighbourhood when the wind's right. All I've got to do is bring one of my plum cakes out of the oven, or a tray of short-bread, or some buns ready for icing. Within a couple of minutes the phone will ring and it will be the vicar or somebody wondering if it would be convenient to pop round.

'Of course,' I say. 'Drop in for tea. I've been baking.' As if they didn't know. Not that I mind, of course. That's what I do it for, isn't it? That's what we're here for, after all. The more the merrier.

I don't do what I call 'posh tea' every day. That's for the special occasion, for people who appreciate a bit of fancy. Weekends, mostly.

When it's just a rough cup round the kitchen table I don't bother getting out the mother-of-pearl-handled cake-knives. But I do expect people to behave properly. Bread and butter first, if you please. That's good preparation for living. As Pop and I know, it takes a bit of time before you can enjoy rich fruit cake. Got to get through some bread and butter first.

Not that there's much wrong with a slice from one of my home-made loaves with our yellow Jersey butter on it. Specially with a dollop of strawberry jam.

Sandwiches? I make a big mountain of dainty ones at the weekends and cut the crusts off for the geese. Tomato, bloater paste, gentleman's relish, cucumber . . . I reckon you can't beat a nice fresh cucumber sandwich, even though it's no more than a mouthful at a time. I leave the cucumber slices soaking in vinegar for a while, with plenty of pepper on them. Pop and me had them for tea at the Ritz in London once. Twenty-five bob, and they only gave us two. 'Blimey!' I told the waiter. 'We'll bring our own next time.'

Scones

I usually make about 16 at a time. Even so, it never seems enough. For that I need:

Around a third of a bag of self-raising flour – about 1lb
Pinch of salt
Two good dollops of butter, that's about 4oz. (It's easier to work with if it's a bit soft, and here's a tip for softening it. Heat up a pudding basin by pouring a kettle of boiling water in it. Leave it until it's heated well through. Empty it and put it over a slab of hard butter. This makes it soft and easy to work with without making it oily, which is what you don't want for this job.)
About two-thirds of a cup of sugar – 4oz
A teacupful of currants or sultanas – 4oz
About ½ pint of soured milk. Or you can use less milk and pop a beaten egg into it.

Get the big mixing bowl, sieve the flour and the salt in, and then start rubbing the butter into the flour with your finger tips. You use a bit of technique here (I go into it a bit more in my chapter on baking). What you need is a light touch, just twitching the fingers gently through the mixture and tossing it about a bit so the air gets in. Don't rub the fat hard in, or you'll get a lot of little pellets and have rock cakes, not scones. What you should end up with is a bowl of light, airy stuff that looks like breadcrumbs.

Then stir in the sugar and the dried fruit. If we plan to eat our scones with clotted cream and strawberry jam I sometimes don't put any fruit in, just leave 'em plain. Don't want too much of a good thing.

Stir in a bit of milk, just enough to bind it all together into a nice soft dough, but not too much. Too much milk and it turns into a sticky mess, sticks to your fingers and wraps itself round the rolling-pin, and then what are you going to do? Well, you can try bunging in a bit more flour to dry it up a bit, but with that the scones are never going to come out nice and light and fluffy. So watch out next time.

Roll the mixture out gently on a floured board, leaving it nice and thick. What do you mean by 'thick'? asks Charlie. I'd say about three-quarters of an inch.

Then stamp out circles with a cutter. I use a wine glass. And all the odd bits left over joined together will probably make another couple of scone shapes.

Bung 'em on a greased baking tin, not too close together – got to give them room to breathe and grow. Then bake them in an oven that's good and hot – hotter than for pastry – about 425°F/220°C/gas mark 7. Leave them until they are nicely risen and golden, about 15 minutes. Just time for a glass of something and a breather.

Shortbread

I make a couple at a time, they'll always keep in the biscuit tin. For that I need eight of my heaped serving-spoons of flour, 12oz. If I can get hold of some rice flour, I use about one-third of that to two-thirds of the ordinary, because it makes the shortbread shorter, more crumbly. You'll also need:

Pinch of salt
½ lb pat of butter – it helps if it's a bit soft
4 heaped serving-spoons of caster sugar – 4oz

Put the flour and the salt in a bowl and then rub in the butter with your fingers, like making pastry. Add the sugar, then carry on working the mixture with your hands into a dough. 'Kneading it,' says Charlie. Right. Carry on until it's all bound together, which takes less time in warm weather than in cold, I find. They say they make a lot of shortbread in Scotland. Must take an age up there.

Cut the lump of dough in half and roll out two rounds on a floured board. I make them about the size of one of my pudding plates (about 7 or 8 inches across) then put them on buttered baking trays.

I like to pretty them up a bit, like the ones you get in those tartan tins at Christmas. So I make a fringe round the edge with my fingers, like I do for the pies, then mark out a cartwheel pattern of six or eight wedges with a knife and prick little holes all over the top with a fork.

It's got to be cooked slow, so it gets nice and crisp inside. That needs a middling oven, about 325°F/170°C/gas mark 3, for about three-quarters of an hour or more, until it's a nice shade of pale gold, the colour of a field of corn at harvest time.

Leave it to cool off, then sprinkle some extra sugar on top, break it into its pieces, and try a bit to see if it's all right.

Plain Cake

Marie Antoinette, she's that Queen we named Mariette after, was very partial to a bit of cake. She told everyone they ought to eat it. I expect it was this cake she had in mind. It's called the Victoria Sandwich, after the Queen we named one of our other daughters after. You should end up with nice, light sandwich cakes. What you put inside is up to you – jam, lemon curd, whipped cream. Sprinkle the top with caster or icing sugar.

I usually make a six-egg lot at a time. That fills four sandwich tins. Or sometimes I make one slab of it, in a big 9-inch square tin I have. I use:

¾ lb of butter – make sure it's nice and soft
12 heaped serving-spoons of caster sugar – ¾ lb
6 eggs
8 heaped serving-spoons of self-raising flour – ¾ lb
Milk

Butter the tins, then cut circles of greaseproof to fit snugly in the bottom of each one. Then butter them again. Beat the butter and the sugar in the big mixing bowl until it's creamy and almost white. It's a job, this. I usually have a sit down for it. Luckily, I can usually bribe the kids to have a go, as long as they can lick the spoon afterwards. Only you've got to watch they don't start licking it before. There's a new electric mixing machine that is supposed to do it, but who needs a machine when you've got kids?

Beat in the eggs, one at a time. If you try beating in too much egg at a time, the mixture can curdle – it sort of shrivels up into something like scrambled egg. You'll never be able to beat in the rest of the eggs if that happens. You can rescue it by beating in a spoonful of the flour you've got ready, but don't expect it to turn out as perfick.

Stir in the flour so you get a nice soft mixture. There's a bit of a trick to knowing if it's soft enough: dig a spoon in the mixture, then hold it up and see if it drops off the end of the spoon. If it drops off easy, it's right. But if it sticks on the spoon, stir in some milk until it comes right. You'll know.

Spread the mixture out in the sandwich tins and bake them in a middling oven – around 350°F/180°C/gas mark 4 – for 20 to 25 minutes. They'll look a good golden colour, but the best way of telling if they are done is to press them with your finger. If they are done, they'll feel springy.

When I am using the big tin to make one big cake, I need a cooler oven or else it'll burn on the outside before it's cooked in the middle. Try it at about 325°F/170°C/gas mark 3 for about one and a quarter hours, then test it the same way.

Let them cool in the tins for a while, then turn them on to cooling racks and sandwich them with what you please.

Plum Cake

Can't say as I know why it's called plum cake. It doesn't have any plums in it, no more than the plum pudding we make at Christmas. I like to make a few of these at a time while I'm at it. So I use smallish tins so that I can get a few in the oven at once. Don't take so long to cook, either.

I use an 8-inch tin for each one. And I line it with two layers of buttered greaseproof to make sure there are no crusty bits on the outside. The kids are good at cutting out the shapes for me so the paper fits snug, leaving a couple of inches coming up over the top. Have ready:

½ lb butter

Same of sugar – about ½ lb. I like to use brown sugar when I can get it. It seems to make the cake moister

4 eggs

Grated rind of an orange, or a lemon if you haven't got an orange

About six heaped serving-spoons of plain flour – ½ lb

2 heaped serving-spoons of rice flour – 2oz – if the village shop's remembered to get it in

1 teaspoon of baking powder

A pinch of salt
About 1lb of dried fruit. I sling in what's in the cupboard, but I suppose I aim to use currants and sultanas for three-quarters of it, with chopped candied peel and glacé cherries for the rest. Can't resist those cherries. I did once pop some prunes in – they're dried plums, after all. A few is all right. Don't overdo it, though, and soak 'em overnight in tea first.

Mix it up like a normal cake, creaming up the butter and sugar until it's as white and soft as you can get it, then beating in the eggs (gently! One at a time) and the orange rind. When that's done you can stir in everything else. It helps to stop the fruit sticking together if you mix it up with the flour beforehand. You want the fruit nice and spread out in the cake, not lying about in lumps.

Put the mixture in the tin and bake it in a low oven – about 325°F/170°C/gas mark 3 – for a good two hours, until it's nice and golden. Test it with a skewer to make sure it's cooked. Then leave it in the tin to cool down.

Meringues

I usually make these in the morning and pop 'em in the warming-drawer of my oven to cook slowly for teatime. But I don't like to mix up more than six egg whites at a time. More than that at once and they don't seem to fluff up so well. That makes about ten. So . . .
6 egg whites, nice fresh ones
Pinch of salt
12 heaped serving-spoons of caster sugar – or half caster, half granulated – ¾ lb

You need a big bowl for this, and make sure it's clean. You won't get the egg whites to fluff up if it isn't.

Put the egg whites in the bowl, add the pinch of salt and then whisk them hard until they are white and fluffy – you should be able to turn the bowl upside down and they won't fall out, though once when I tried that I had the lot on the floor. One Christmas the twins gave me a posh new electric egg-whisk which stiffens 'em up really well. Thank you very much, I said. I suppose this means you want more meringues for tea. But I still give them a last go with my hand whisk. The final bit of elbow grease makes all the difference.

Then whisk in the sugar a spoonful at a time. Whisk it well each time, it'll get thicker and whiter as you go on. Spoon big dollops of it on to greaseproof lined, buttered baking trays and cook in a really low oven for hours until they're nice and dry. You don't want 'em to get brown. They'll lift off the trays when they're ready.

Sandwich them together with plenty of cream that has been whipped up with a spot of fine sugar.

Iced Buns

I get fresh yeast from the bakers for these, but I suppose you could use the dried stuff that comes in tins. Remember to keep all the bowls and everything a bit warm when dealing with yeast. It doesn't like cold and draughts any more than I do. These ingredients will make about 15.
8 heaped serving spoons of bread flour – ¾ lb
Pinch of salt
A good dollop of butter – about 2oz
1-2 heaped serving-spoons of caster sugar – 1-2oz
Knob of fresh yeast – about ½ oz
About ½ pint of warm water to mix the yeast in. It should be just hot enough so your little finger can stay in it

Crumble the yeast into half the water and leave for ten minutes or so. It should get frothy, like the top of a Guinness.

Meanwhile, mix the flour and salt and then rub in the butter with your fingertips, the way I showed you with scones. Then stir in the sugar.

Mix the yeasty liquid into the flour and make a nice, smooth dough. It shouldn't be at all sticky, so it's best to go carefully and use three-quarters of the water first, adding the rest a bit at a time until it's just right.

I love this bit. You get your lump of dough, put it on a floured board, and give it a good going over, a real pummelling, for about ten minutes. Slap it about until it is as smooth as a baby's whatsit, just like the skin on our Oscar. Then cover it with a cloth and leave it somewhere cosy and warm for about half an hour (the dough, silly, not our Oscar). You'll find it will have grown to about twice its size. Give it another going over on the board (funny, the way it shrinks when you touch it) and leave it to rise for another half an hour or so.

Roll it into balls and put it on buttered baking trays. You'll have to space them well apart, because they will keep on growing. Cover them with a clean tea-towel until they are twice as big as they were when you started. Then they are ready for the oven. You need it really hot right from the start – about 450°F/230°C/gas mark 8 – to kill off the yeast. Otherwise the buns would swell up and start breaking down the oven door to get out. They turn a nice golden colour, and you should leave them in until they're done, could be 15 or 20 minutes. How do you know when they're ready? Pick one up and give it a tap on the bottom. If it sounds hollow, it's ready.

When they're cold, spoon a bit of icing on top. I mix sifted icing sugar with some water and a squeeze of lemon juice until it's quite thick, then dollop a spoonful on top of each bun.

ANY EXCUSE FOR A PARTY

Any excuse for a party with us. I love going to 'em. So I suppose it's natural I should love giving 'em. The old General said to me once: 'You've got the secret of entertaining.' I don't know about that. As far as I know if you give a crowd of people enough to eat and drink the entertaining will look after itself.

I remember one of our parties, after the gymkhana, the year they held it in our meadow. Charlie decided it was going to be a cocktail party, so he got out a book with advice in it about what to give everyone. Had it all down, how many chocolate éclairs, how many lettuces for the salads, how many bottles of champagne. That was a laugh, 'For a party of 50 people,' it said, 'you'll need 50 sausage rolls.' Blimey, one each? Pop and me usually get through half a dozen even before the guests come. For drink it said, 'Ten bottles of champagne or other wine.' One glass and that's your lot! Funny kind of party that would have been. So we chucked the book away after that and just carried on with what we thought best. Everyone seemed to enjoy themselves.

To Roast a Chicken

Whether you have this cold for a party or hot for your dinner, you cook it the same way. One will be enough for four people if it's hot, as long as it has all the trimmings – little sausages and bacon rolls and bread sauce. For a party I usually carve it up and serve with a whole lot of other cold meats.

We mostly kill our own. After they've hung for a couple of days I do the drawing and plucking and trussing. But if you get one from the butcher, you just need to wipe out the insides with a damp cloth. Then I stick an onion and a knob of butter with a few herbs from the garden inside – that helps give it some extra flavour and keeps it moist while it's cooking.

I usually put a bit of mild-flavoured forcemeat stuffing in the neck end (I'll tell you how I make that afterwards), but not too much or it'll ooze out when it's cooking. Make sure the skin at the neck end is big enough to wrap under the bird, then stick in a skewer to hold it in place. Brush the bird with melted butter and sprinkle it with salt and pepper. I usually lay a few rashers of fatty bacon on top for extra flavour and to keep it moist.

An average bird will take about $1\frac{1}{2}$ to 2 hours in a medium hot oven, 375-400°F/190-200°C/gas mark 5-6. I got a tip once about how to keep the white meat even more moist and tasty: start off cooking the bird upside down, then all the juices from the legs run down into the breast. You can turn it on both sides for a while, as well. And then give the last half-hour or so breast-side up to get the skin crisp and golden. You need to baste it every now and again as well, of course.

How do you know if it's done? Just stick a skewer or a fork into the thick part of the thigh. If the juice comes out clear, it's done. If there's a bit of blood colour about it, it needs a bit longer. Don't forget to drain off any juices before putting it on the plate.

Forcemeat Stuffing

You can stuff any light, mild-flavoured meat, like chicken or rabbit, with this:

A bit of suet – about 2oz
About the same weight of ham or bacon
2 teacups of breadcrumbs – about 4oz
Bunch of parsley
A few mixed herbs from the garden
Rind of half a lemon
Salt and pepper
Beaten egg

Chop the suet and the ham or bacon really fine and mix in a bowl with the breadcrumbs. Add all the herbs, the lemon rind and a pinch of salt and pepper. Add just enough beaten egg to bind it all together, then get stuffing, if you'll pardon the expression.

To Roast Duck

There's not much meat on a duck, but I do love the taste. An average duck weighs 4-5lb when it's cleaned and that's really just enough for two or three people. So I usually cook three to be on the safe side.

I give the bird a good wipe inside and out with a damp cloth, then stick an onion and a quartered orange inside, with a few sprigs of herbs from the garden. Prick it all over with a fork, to let the fat get out from under the skin, then sprinkle it with salt and pepper and rub it in a bit. You'll want to raise the duck on a bit of a trivet when you put it in the roasting tin. A lot of fat comes out of a duck and you don't want it swimming in it.

I prefer roasting it in a medium hot oven – 350°F/180°C/gas mark 4 – for about two hours, until the skin is really crisp. You can see whether it's cooked the usual way for birds, stick a skewer in the thick part of the leg and see if the juice runs clear. Take it off the trivet and drain the juice out of the inside of the body. If it's for cold I dress it up with some orange slices and watercress. Hot it's good with a bit of sage and onion stuffing (put into the tail end) and apple sauce. And don't forget the fresh green peas.

To Roast Turkey

It's the same kind of a job as a chicken, really. But because it's bigger it's got to be cooked slower and longer. Our turkeys come out at about 14-16lb when they are cleaned up and ready for the oven. We keep the black-feathered ones. Got a better flavour than the white ones, though they are a bit of a fiddle to pluck properly. Definitely worth the trouble, though.

Wipe the bird inside and out with a damp cloth as usual. I normally stuff the neck end with sausage meat or a sausage meat stuffing (fry up some pork sausage meat and chopped onion in a bit of dripping, then mix with parsley, herbs and breadcrumbs). Then wrap the flap of neckskin under the bird and fix it with a skewer. Stick a couple of onions and a few sprigs of herbs inside the hole at the back, with a good dollop of butter.

Start it off upside down in the oven, so all the juices run down into the breast for the first two hours of cooking. Give it a good going over with melted butter and sprinkle it with salt and pepper. I cook it fairly slow, in a medium oven, about 325-350°F/170-180°C/gas mark 3-4. After two hours, basting it every now and then, I turn it over and give it another couple of hours breast-side up. If the skin still isn't crisp and brown, turn up the oven and give it a final blast. Got to keep basting all the time, though, to keep it moist. Nothing worse than dried-up turkey meat, specially if you're having it cold.

Test it like the other birds, with a skewer in the thigh. It sometimes happens that the skin starts to brown before the bird is properly cooked inside. In that case turn the oven back down again and carry on cooking until the juices run clear. You can cover the breast with a bit of greaseproof if you think it's scorching. Got to keep an eye on it.

For a party I take it out of the tin and leave it to go cold in a cool place, then I stick a whole bunch of fresh herbs on it to posh it up a bit.

To Cook a Gammon

Meat always seems to taste better on the bone. But a gammon's definitely more difficult to carve that way. So you'll have to please yourself whether you bone it or not. If you do have the bone out, make sure you get the meat tied into a good shape with string.

I cure our ham and bacon myself. So I know that when I use my sweet-cure mixture and hang the joint from a hook in a cotton bag for six months, it isn't going to be so salty as to need soaking before cooking, but if you haven't cured it yourself, you won't know where you are with saltiness. So it's best to be on the safe side and put it in a pan of cold water and just bring it to the boil, then throw away the first lot of water. If you've got plenty of time, you can soak it overnight in cold water.

A whole gammon will weigh about a stone or more, so it's good for a party – plenty to cut at. Needs a huge pan, though. Unless you've got one, you are probably better off using a large piece off the bone. A good-sized piece would be 6-8lb. That'll take 2-3 hours to cook. For a plain boiled ham I often cook it in cider. Put the joint in a large pan and cover half with cider and half with water. Add a few cloves and peppercorns and bring it to the boil.

When it's boiling, cover the pan and simmer it gently for about two hours. Then lift it out of the pan and leave it to cool for a bit. Peel off the skin and make a pattern on the top with a sharp knife, cutting diagonal lines in opposite directions to make diamond shapes. You can stick a clove in each diamond.

Now comes the clever bit. You've got a choice. Put the meat in a roasting tin and either cover it with brown sugar, or – for something a bit special – brush it with honey or marmalade. Then bake it in a medium oven – 350°F/ 180°C/gas mark 4 – for another one hour or so, until the meat feels really tender when you test it with a skewer or fork. Cut a sliver off and have a taste to be sure.

For a party leave it to go cold and have it nestling in a bed of watercress. You get that hint of something spicy and special from the cloves, the cider and the honey coating. Eats sweet as a nut.

To Cook an Ox Tongue

I can't say I'm all that partial to hot tongue. On a plate, I mean. But it's smashing cold with other meats and salads – specially beetroot, or something tangy like cucumber pickle.

I always cook two together. Then I can press them into a tin so that they set into a nice firm round that you can cut into. You need:

2 ox tongues – the butcher gets me cured ones
A couple of onions
A couple of carrots
A couple of sticks of celery
A couple of bay leaves
A handful of other herbs – I usually have thyme, parsley and tarragon in the summer
A few peppercorns and cloves

You need a really big pan for this. Cover the tongues with cold water and bring them to the boil. Then drain off the water – that gets rid of some of the saltiness. I'm not sure our village butcher has got his curing mixture quite right.

Cover with cold water again and add everything else – you'll need to chop up the veg. Bring to the boil, then simmer until the tongues are really tender. Let's see, if I put them on first thing, when Pop's just gone off after his first breakfast, I can have them skinned and into the tin before dinner-time – so that'll be about 4–5 hours' cooking.

Leave them to cool, then pour off the water and skin them. Make sure you take out any small bones and gristly bits, then curl the tongues into a small tin. I use a round 7-inch baking tin. They fit really snug in that. Put a plate on top, press it down with a weight and pop it in the fridge overnight.

Cold Poached Salmon

I am not so fussed about hot salmon. But I do like a nice cold salmon, and it can look really posh for a party. Should do, too, at what some shops are charging for them these days. Last time Pop phoned up Harrods to ask the price, he had to tell 'em he wanted to buy a salmon, not a bloomin' salmon river.

I've tried baking them in the oven. But poaching seems better, keeps them nice and moist. It's horrible if it dries up. What you do need is a good-sized pan to cook it in. I've got a proper old fish kettle, long and thin, like the fish, with a rack in it to keep the fish off the bottom.

If it's me clean-ing the salmon, I make sure I get all the dark bits of blood out of the belly. And I cut out the gills at the back of the head underneath those flap things, because they can give it a bad taste. Then I put it in the pan and cover it with water. But I learned long ago that it must be well-salted water, like seawater. I've got a mixture for it – 3oz of salt to 7 pints of water – and that's usually enough to cover the fish nicely. Then all you have to do is heat the water up to boiling point. But as soon as you see the first bubble blooping up to show it's boiling, turn off the heat and leave it to go cold. Nothing to it. But it comes out perfick every time.

When it's cold I take the skin off and decorate it up with cucumber slices on top and lettuce round the edges.

When the asparagus is in season there's nothing nicer to eat salmon with than that. We get the thin, tender green stuff round here. There's hardly any of the coarse white bit to cut off. One of the growers showed me a good way of cooking it. You just lay it out flat in a roasting tin, pour boiling salted water on top of it and simmer it on top of the stove until you can feel the stems are tender. It goes a lovely bright green colour and only takes a few minutes to be ready. He likes to support the tips just out of the water on a pillow of folded foil or something similar, because they cook quicker than the stems and can get mushy and fall to pieces if you don't watch out.

Salads

It's a bit difficult for me to say what I do for party salads. I do something different every time, makin' 'em up as I go along. The main thing is, they got to look a bit unusual and exciting. And they have got to have a good dressing on them. Keep some chopped fresh herbs to sprinkle over them, as well. As I keep telling you, what looks good, eats good.

Course, they've got to look fresh. Don't want any of that old, tired lettuce, limp as a docker's collar. We mostly get ours crisp from the garden, but I'll tell you what we used to do with a tired lettuce at the Three Cocks – let it soak in water with a bit of coal in it. Soon crisps it up. Don't ask me why.

So here are four of my regulars:

Tomato

Cut the tomatoes into wedges (taking that hard bit of core out) and sprinkle with chopped spring onion and mustard and cress, or chopped parsley.

Beetroot

Good one for winter. Quarter some baby pickled beetroot and mix with chopped eating apples and sliced celery.

Watercress

Mix the sprigs up with sliced cucumber. Or slice up some oranges, then mix them up with the watercress. Nice if you've got some cold duck or pheasant.

Potato

Mix some cold chopped new potatoes with sliced radishes and chopped spring onions. Mix it all up with salad cream and sprinkle it with parsley.

Cheese Straws

As we always dunk these in Worcestershire sauce, I thought I'd try putting some in a mixture to see what happened. Gives it a nice tang.

To make about 50 you need:

8 heaped serving-spoons of plain flour – ¾ lb
A good sprinkling of dry mustard
Salt and pepper
3 big dollops of butter – 6oz
2 good handfuls of grated Cheddar – ½ lb

1-2 eggs (or use one egg and a couple of tablespoons of milk)
2 tablespoons of Worcestershire sauce

Mix the flour and the mustard and add plenty of salt and pepper. Then rub in the butter lightly with your fingers, like you do for pastry, and stir in the cheese. Beat up the eggs (or egg and milk) with the Worcestershire sauce and use the liquid to mix up a nice stiff dough.

Roll it out into an oblong shape and cut out some nice fat fingers of dough. If I've got time, I make them look pretty by twisting 'em.

They need to be baked on a buttered tray in a hot oven – about 425°F/ 220°C/ gas mark 7 – for about 15 minutes, when they should be nice and golden.

Sausage Rolls

You can make these any size you like. For the gymkhana party I cut them quite small, because people standing talking want something to wolf down in one mouthful. But for a late-night snack in front of the telly I make big fat ones – perfick dipped in tomato ketchup. To make about 30 party types you'll need:

1lb of puff pastry (see my baking bit)
2lb of sausage meat

Roll out the pastry nice and thin on your floured board. Cut it into long strips, but make the strips wide enough to wrap round your sausage meat.

Now roll the sausage meat into long sausegey lengths, just like the strips of pastry. Then lay the meat down the middle of the pastry lengths. Brush the pastry with beaten egg or milk so that it will stick together, then wrap it round your sausage meat. Make all the edges of the pastry neat and make sure they're stuck down well. You don't want the meat bursting out of them while they're in the oven.

Cut up the long rolls into pieces, whatever length you fancy, and make a couple of slanting slashes in the top of each one with the point of a knife. Brush with some beaten egg or milk to give 'em a bit of a shine and bake for about half an hour. You start them off in a hot oven – about 425°F/220°C/gas mark 7 – to get the pastry nice and crisp. Then turn it down to about 350°F/180°C/gas mark 4 for the last 15 minutes to make sure the sausage meat is cooked right through.

Kent Apple Tart

This used to go down a treat with the visitors from Town when I had it on the menu at the Three Cocks, the pub my mum and dad used to keep in Fordington. People used to ask, 'What's Kentish about it?' The apples, I told 'em. Made from our own big, green Bramleys. Can't beat them for taste.

About 10-12oz shortcrust pastry – you need enough to line one of my larger-sized pie-plates, not as deep as a dish
1 egg
A good dollop of butter – about 2oz
About 4 heaped serving-spoons of sugar – 4oz – doesn't really matter what sort
Grated rind and juice of 1 lemon
2 large Bramleys, grated

Roll out the pastry and use it to line the pie-plates. I usually do a fancy raised pattern round the edge with my fingers. It doesn't just look pretty, it stops the filling oozing over. Beat the egg, butter and sugar together then stir in the lemon and apples. Pour it all onto the pastry and bake in a medium hot oven – about 375°F/190°C/gas mark 5 – for a good 45 minutes or more, probably nearly an hour, until the grated apple is nice and golden.

Sugar Crusted Apple Pie

I love apples just like this. But I have known folk who layer it up with slices of cheese, as well. The one in Charlie's snap above uses blackberries, too.

About 1¼–1½ lb of shortcrust pastry – enough to line and cover my big pie-plate
4-6 Bramleys
White sugar
Egg white

Roll out half the pastry and line the pie-plate – I honestly prefer my old tin jobs to the new-fangled heat-proof glass. The pastry gets nice and crisp cooked on metal, specially if you rub it with a buttered paper first.

Peel, core and slice the apples and pile them (with blackberries if you're using 'em) as high as you can on the pastry – they don't half shrink a lot when they are cooking – sprinkling them with sugar every now and then. I get through about 3 heaped serving-spoons of sugar in each pie. Roll out the rest of the pastry and use it to cover the apples.

Don't forget to wet the edges so it sticks together. Trim the edges and make a pretty fringe with your fingers or a fork. Make a couple of fork marks in the top to let the steam out or else it probably split and spill juice all over the shop. Brush the top of the pastry with the egg white, then sprinkle it with lots of sugar.

Bake it in a hot oven – about 400°F/200°C/gas mark 6 – for 20-30 minutes. Then turn it down to about 350°F/180°C/gas mark 4 and cook until the pastry is golden and the fruit inside is nice and soft, another half-hour or so. I stick a small knife or a sharp metal skewer in the top to test it.

BAKING DAY

They say that all you need to make pastry is cool fingers and a hot oven. There's a good bit more to it than that, but not much. I don't know why some people make such a fuss over it. It's easy when you get the hang. Practice makes perfect.

There are some things you have to watch, though. I know my faults by now, and one of them is being a bit rough and ready with my quantities (you've probably picked that up already). I tend to slap in as much of something as I feel like at the time. Well you can't be like that with pastry. My usual guesswork's no use, either. In fact it's become a bit of a joke with our lot. When they see me get my old scales with the lead weights down from the top shelf they all say, 'Hello – it must be Ma's baking day'.

Because if you want to end up with a pastry that's light, crisp and makes your mouth water just to look at it, then you've got to get the ingredients right. And yes, you've got to keep it all cool as well. On hot days I keep a jug of water handy in the fridge for the liquid. For rolling out I've got a nice bit of marble counter top that Pop got for a quid from the village shop when they went over to one of those new cool cabinets.

Most often I make two kinds – shortcrust and puff. Shortcrust is my favourite for most things, although there's nothing to beat a crisp hot puff on top of a steak and kidney pie.

Shortcrust Pastry

Shortcrust is the easiest. I make a big batch at a time for all my tarts and pies.

Take **a bag of plain flour – 3lb** – and sift it into your big mixing-bowl with **plenty of salt** (two or three teaspoons for this amount, depending on your taste). Then you need exactly **half the weight of fat to flour**. I use lard and butter – lard makes it crumbly and butter gives it flavour. So, $1^{1}/_{2}$lb altogether, chopped up into little bits. It shouldn't be rock hard, just softened slightly.

Now comes a bit of technique. You've got to rub the little bits of fat into the flour. I take some in each hand, rubbing the fat and the flour together between my thumb and forefinger without being too heavy-handed about it. It's a gesture I've seen Pop make when he's talking about money. Keep it all light and airy, tossing it about a bit.

When you've rubbed all the fat and flour together you should end up with something like breadcrumbs, evenly mixed but not stuck together.

Then comes the tricky bit – adding the water. You'll soon learn how much you need. The worst thing is to put in too much, so that the mixture becomes wet and sticky. What you want is a mixture that is firm and soft. So I start by sprinkling in a teacupful and pulling the mixture together with my fingers. Then I add a little bit at a time until it feels right. If it's too dry it won't roll out properly. If it's too wet it sticks to everything and you'll have to add more flour. But that'll mean your balance of ingredients won't be right and the pastry will come out a bit tough and hard when it's baked.

Puff Pastry

A bit of a fiddle, this. But worth it in the end. Start off by making the same mixture as for your shortcrust, but only rub in a quarter of your fat (it helps if you start off by dividing your fat into four quarters). Mix in the water carefully as before, but also squeeze in some lemon juice which toughens it up a bit and makes it easier to roll out.

Roll it out into an oblong, take another quarter of your creamed-up fat and dot that in little flakes evenly over two-thirds of the surface of the pastry, leaving the other third bare. Got that? Now sprinkle it with a bit of flour and fold it as though it were a bedsheet, the bottom third (which is bare, remember) up to the middle and the top third down to the middle.

You've got a little oblong parcel now. Turn it round on your board so it's lengthways-on to you and roll it out into a big oblong again. Go through the whole flaking, folding and turning lark twice more, using the two remaining quarters of fat.

After giving it a final roll I fold it again, wrap the parcel in greaseproof and a cloth that's slightly damp and leave it somewhere cool for a bit. If I can remember I like to make it the evening before I want to use it for my pies. It handles easier and comes out better for resting overnight.

When they are cooked they'll be a beautiful sight to behold, lovely and risen and golden brown. They should come out of the tin easily. Tap the bottom of the loaf with your knuckles and it should sound hollow if it's properly cooked. Leave it to cool on a wire tray.

Bread

If I find myself getting at all riled up about anything, I'll make some bread. I don't know why it is, but it always makes me feel better. I suppose it's because the dough has such a lovely feel to it. And you can really lay into it – the rougher the better. The more I've got a mood on, the nicer the bread turns out. Well, did you ever meet a bad-tempered baker?

I make mine in tins, but you can make them any shape you like – round cobs or plaited loaves look good on the table. You need to use what they call strong flour, or bread flour.

For every bag of flour – 3lb – you need:
A serving-spoon of salt – about 1oz
A knob of lard – about 1oz
A knob of fresh yeast – about 1oz (I get fresh yeast from the baker. It doesn't keep more than a day or two, so you won't need much at a time. It's no use when it gets dry and crumbly. Of course you can use the dried yeast, following the instructions on the packet.)
About 1¼ pints of warm water. It's got to be warm enough to get the yeast going, but cool enough for you to keep your little finger in it. Blood heat, you'd call it. Too hot and the yeast will sulk or even give up the ghost.

Mix the flour and the salt in a large mixing bowl and rub in the lard. Mix the yeast with the water and leave it in a warm place till it froths like a good beer. Then mix the yeasty liquid into the flour and start the kneading. Give it a good going over for about ten minutes until it's smooth and stretchy, but not sticky, on a lightly floured board and pummel away, turning it round as you work.

Put it in a greased bowl, cover it with a clean tea-towel and leave it in a warm place. It'll start rising. You are supposed to let it double in size, which can take half an hour to an hour, depending on how warm your kitchen is.

Then you have to knead it some more. Put it on your lightly floured board and cut it in half. Give each piece another going over until it's nice and smooth again. Then put it in a greased loaf tin – one of the large ones – to rise again. Cover them with the clean tea-towel and after a while they will have risen once again to about double the size.

That's the time to put them in a hot oven to kill the yeast and stop them rising any more. The temperature should be about 450°F/230°C/gas mark 8 and they'll take about 40 minutes.

Quiche Lorraine

This is one I got from Mme Dupont when we had a holiday in her hotel, just after Oscar was born. Except for the fancy French cheese they use, it's much like the cheese and bacon tart I've always made. Between you and me – I grate up any old cheese I've got left. But you've got to admit that asking someone if they'd like a slice of Quiche Lorraine sounds a rung up from offering them a bit of cheese tart. I use:
Enough pastry for my big 10-inch pie dish – about ¾lb of shortcrust. Don't waste the trimmings. They're good for making little tarts
A piece of bacon – about ½lb – chopped up small. (It makes a good handful when chopped)
A knob of butter – about 1oz
A good handful of grated cheese – 3-4oz. You can miss this out if you like, but use 1 pint of cream instead of ¾ pint if you do
4 eggs
¾ pint of fresh cream – you can use milk, but it tastes much better with cream
Salt, pepper and nutmeg. I sometimes add a sprinkling of herbs from the garden

Roll out the pastry and line the pie dish with it. Press the edges well down to stop them falling into the custard mix when it's cooking. Spoil the effect, that would.

Fry the bacon in the butter – I always taste a bit to test how salty it is – and put it in the dish with the cheese. Beat the eggs and cream together and add salt – depending on the bacon – and pepper and a big pinch of nutmeg. Pour this custard mix on top of the bacon and cheese and bake for about 45 minutes in a fairly hot oven – about 375–400°F/190–200°C/gas mark 5-6.

Keep an eye on it while it's cooking. If you catch it getting too brown before the custard's set properly turn the oven down about 50°F and keep on cooking until it's set. Or you could swap it down to the bottom of the oven, where it's cooler.

Open Cheese Tart

I use the same big 10-inch pie dish for this tart and decorate it up with some of the tinned anchovies that I have to go up to London to find.

Shortcrust pastry to line the dish – about ¾ lb
1 large onion – mine weigh about ½ lb – chopped. Or you can chop up some leeks instead
A big knob of butter – about 1oz
A good handful of grated cheese – about 4oz
4 eggs
¾ pint of fresh cream
Salt and pepper
A small tin of anchovies – if they are very salty I soak them in water for a while

Line the pie dish with pastry, pressing the edges down well. Fry the onion in butter until it's soft, then put in the pie dish with the cheese. Beat the eggs and the cream with salt and pepper – less salt if you are using the anchovies – and pour it into the dish. Arrange a cartwheel of anchovies on top. Bake it for about the same time as the Quiche Lorraine, and don't forget the tip about the baking tray.

Apple and Apricot Flan

I've got a special flan dish for this – about 10 inches across. It needs about ¾ lb of **shortcrust pastry** to line it, then for the rest:

4 medium Bramleys
4 heaped serving-spoons of sugar – about 4oz – doesn't matter what sort
2 serving-spoons of water – enough to stop the apples sticking to the pan
1 tablespoon of arrowroot
10 large fresh apricots
Apricot jam

Roll out the pastry and line the flan dish. Prick the bottom with a fork, making plenty of holes. Then put in a sheet of greaseproof and some of the dried beans I use for holding the pastry in shape while baking cases for flans and tarts, and cook it in a hot oven – about 400°F/200°C/ gas mark 6 – for 20 minutes or so.

You know the technique – you take the beans and the paper out once the pastry edges have set at 'half time', so the pastry can dry out on the bottom. You can turn the oven down a bit – by about 25°F – after that.

While all that's cooking, you can deal with the apples. Slice them and put them in a pan with the sugar and water and cook gently until the apple is fairly soft. Mix the arrowroot with a splash of water and stir it into the apples – that thickens up nicely as it cooks.

You have to leave this mixture to cool a bit, then put it in the pastry case. Cut the apricots in half, take the stones out and sink them down – cut side up – into the apple. Press them down a bit so they sink in well. Put a dollop of jam in the middle of each apricot, then pop it in the oven for about 30 minutes until

the apricots are soft (I stick a skewer in them to check) and just browned slightly.

Apricot Flan

Make the pastry case and bake it with the beans in the same way as you do for the Apple and Apricot Flan.
For this filling you need:
2lb fresh apricots
4 heaped serving-spoons of sugar –
4oz – of any sort
2 serving-spoons of water
2 tablespoons of arrowroot
1-2 heaped serving-spoons of ground almonds or breadcrumbs – 1-2oz

Quarter the apricots and cook them with sugar and water until just soft. Mix the arrowroot with a splash of water and mix into the apricots – as it cooks it'll thicken. Let it cool a bit.

Sprinkle some ground almonds in the pastry case and pour the apricot mixture on top. The almonds will soak up some of the juice. Bake in a hot oven – about 400°F/200°C/gas mark 6 – for about 20 minutes or so, until you see the apricots just getting a tinge of brown colour.

Curd Tarts

I usually make little tarts. But if you like you can use the same amount of filling, but less pastry, to make one big tart, 10-inch-pie plate size.

These ingredients make about two dozen:
Enough shortcrust pastry to line 2 trays of bun tins – about 1lb
A good dollop of butter – about 2oz
2 heaped serving-spoons of sugar – about 2oz
1 heaped serving-spoon of ground almonds or bread-crumbs – about 1oz
2 eggs
1½ teacups of curds or cottage cheese – ¾lb
Juice of half a lemon
3 heaped serving-spoons of currants – 3oz
Nutmeg

Roll out the pastry and stamp out pastry rounds to fit your two trays of bun tins.

Make sure the butter is soft, then beat everything together with a wooden spoon until it is well mixed. Spoon this mixture into the little pastry cases and sprinkle each one with a little ground nutmeg.

Bake in a hot oven – about 375–400°F/190–200°C/gas mark 5-6 – until it is set and golden-coloured. That takes around 25 minutes. If you are doing a big tart, it will take longer – about three-quarters of an hour.

Treacle Tart

For this one you'll need:

Enough shortcrust pastry to line a large pie-plate – about ¾ lb
6 serving-spoons of golden syrup – about ¾ lb
2 heaped serving-spoons of ground almonds – 2oz
3 heaped serving-spoons of fresh breadcrumbs – 3oz
Grated rind and juice of half a lemon
1 egg
3 serving-spoons of fresh cream

Roll out the pastry on a floured board and line a large pie plate with it. Mix everything else and pour it into the pastry case.

Bake in a medium hot oven – 375°F/190°C/gas mark 5 – until the pastry is a nice golden brown and the filling is set and golden as well.

Dough Cakes

When my grandma made these she called them Kentish Huffkins.
For every bag of bread flour – 3lb – you will need:
1 tablespoon of salt
2 good dollops of lard – 4oz
A large knob of fresh yeast – 1oz
A couple of teaspoons of sugar
About 1½ pints of milk and water

Sift the flour and the salt in a bowl and rub in the lard until you can't see it any more. Mix up the yeast and the sugar in some of the warm liquid (finger hot, as for the bread dough) and leave it to froth up in a warm place for 10-15 minutes. Then mix everything together until it's a nice soft dough, but not sticky.

Put it on a floured board and give it a good kneading for ten minutes or so – the longer the better. You want it soft and smooth like a baby's skin. Then leave it covered with a cloth in a bowl in a warm place for about an hour. It will grow to about twice its size.

Knead it again, then cut your lump of dough into about 16 bits and knead each one into a ball. Then flatten them with your hand until they are about an inch thick. Put them on greased baking trays and cover with a clean tea-towel. You need to put them fairly wide apart, because they are going to spread a bit. Leave them to rise for another 20-30 minutes, then make a dent with your thumb in the middle of each one and bake in an oven that's good and hot – about 450°F/230°C/gas mark 8 – for 20 minutes or so, turning them over half-way through. If they sound hollow when you tap them, they're cooked.

To keep them soft I wrap them in a tea-towel while they cool.

At the end of a bout of this lark, you'll have flour in your hair and odd trimmings of pastry all over the kitchen. That's when you can sit down, pour yourself a glass of something and take a whiff of the one perfume that I've found never fails to get people going – the smell of baking.

Stocking Up the Larder

You get that nip in the clear evening air which tells you that summer is ending. And there's something else in the air round about then which tells me the same thing – the smell of pickling vinegar.

I don't know what it is about a row of home-made pickles, jams and chutneys in the storecupboard. They make you feel secure, like a trunkful of money – whatever happens, you won't starve. And you're never short of something to give people as presents.

The kids usually make fun of me round about this time: 'If it doesn't move, Ma'll pickle it.' Well, they do all right out of it, down on their stall, selling pickles to the motorists. It doesn't just start with the Autumn, of course. There's spare fruit like the redcurrants and the gooseberries to be dealt with all summer. And some things, like the walnuts from our tree, are best used when they are still on the under-ripe side in July or August. But September and October is when it all gets hectic. There are boxes of windfall apples lying about the pantry. There are baskets of blackberries, all those green tomatoes, the lovely red cabbages, and we always have more runner beans and cauliflowers than even our family can eat. And having four or five crisp pickles to choose from cheers up a plate of cold no end.

Well, at least we found something to do with those army surplus gherkins Pop got lumbered with. Didn't have much use for the gherkins. But the jars have turned out a godsend.

Apple Chutney

6-8 largish Bramleys – about 4lb
1 pint of malt vinegar
1 large onion
About 1½ packets of brown sugar – 1½lb
2 teaspoons of ground ginger
Half a teaspoon of mixed spice
A good pinch of salt
A pinch of cayenne pepper

Peel, core and chop the apples, and cook them in a big jam-pan with half the vinegar and the chopped onion until they're pulpy. Add the rest of the things and cook until the mixture is nice and thick.

You have to keep stirring so that it doesn't start sticking to the bottom of the pan. There's a way of telling when it's ready – take a wooden spoon and drag it along the bottom of the pan through the mixture; if it makes a parting and you can see a clean line of metal across the bottom, it's ready. Pop into clean, hot jars and cover with vinegar-proof paper.

Mixed Fruit Chutney

This is good for using up any fruits, like green tomatoes, pears, plums and apples.
2-3 medium onions, about 1lb
3lb of mixed fruit, whatever you like
A good handful of dates – 4oz
1 teaspoon of salt
1 teaspoon of mixed spices
1 teaspoon of dry mustard
1lb packet of brown sugar
1 pint of malt vinegar

Chop the onion up small, then chop all the fruit. You'll have to peel and core apples and pears and take the stones out of things like plums.

Put everything into a jam-pan and bring it to the boil, then simmer until the chutney goes thick, it could take about three quarters of an hour or more. Keep stirring so it doesn't stick and do my test with the wooden spoon dragged along the bottom to see when it's thick enough to pot.

Put it in clean hot jars and top with the vinegar-proof paper. Leave the covering and labelling until its cooled down.

Pickled Walnuts

It always seems a shame not to do something worthwhile with the walnuts off our tree. But they must be young and green for pickling, before the hard shell has formed. I poke a needle through them to make sure.

You just wash them and put them in a big bowl of cold salt water – about 1lb of salt to every gallon of water. The best way to dissolve the salt is to warm it up in a small pan of water, then add it to the rest and leave it to go cold. For salt water it needs to be a glass or china bowl, of course.

Leave the walnuts to soak for a week, then drain them and soak them in a fresh lot of salt water for another week. Then you drain them again and leave them on trays in a dry airy place for a couple of days until they go black. Once they've done that you just put them in jars, cover them with vinegar, seal the jars and don't forget to label them. After about two months you can start eating them.

Beetroot Pickle

6 medium beetroots
Just over ½ pint of vinegar – about 12fl oz
1½ tablespoons of dry mustard
Half a teaspoon of salt
A good half pound of sugar – more like 9-10oz
2 medium onions

Cook the beetroots in boiling water until they are soft, and keep about ½ pint of the cooking water. Peel and slice the beetroot when they are cool enough to touch.

Boil up the vinegar with the water you've kept, plus the mustard, salt and sugar. Give it a good stir, then boil it up again.

Slice the onions thinly, then make layers of them with the sliced beetroot in jars. Cover it with the hot vinegar mixture.

Screw the top of the jars on tight as you can and leave in a cool place for at least a week before being tempted to try a bit.

Pickled Onions

About 4 lb of the small pickling onions
About 4 serving-spoons of salt – 4½ oz
1½ pints of water
2 pints of malt vinegar
4 serving-spoons of sugar – 4oz

Peel the onions and leave them to soak in the salt and water for 24 hours. Rinse them well, then shake them dry in a big sieve or colander. Pack them tightly into jars and fill the jars up with vinegar.

I like a bit of sweetness to them, so I melt the sugar into some of the vinegar in a small pan and then add it to the rest before pouring it over the onions.

They are ready to eat in two weeks, but they'll keep for six months, I believe. Not in this house!

Gooseberry Chutney

1 big onion – about ½ lb
4lb gooseberries
About ¾ of a packet of raisins – ¾ lb
¾ of a bag of sugar – 1½ lb
1 tablespoon of salt
2 tablespoons of ground ginger
A good pinch of cayenne pepper
1 pint of malt vinegar

Chop the onion up quite small, then put it in a jam-pan with all the other ingredients and bring it to the boil. Simmer it for three-quarters of an hour or more until it's thick, stirring every now and then to make sure it doesn't stick. You'll know with my wooden-spoon trick, drawing it along the bottom of the pan to see if you can see the line clearly.

Pot it into hot clean jars when it's done. Cover it with the vinegar-proof paper and leave it to cool before covering it and labelling it.

Redcurrant Jelly

Don't know how we could enjoy the lamb and the game without it . . .
4lb redcurrants
1 pint of water
Sugar

You have to make the juice first. So put the redcurrants – stalks, leaves and all – into a jam-pan with the water and simmer for about 45 minutes after you've brought it to the boil, until the fruit is really soft. You can try it with a wooden spoon.

What you need now is a jelly bag. Just let the pulp drip through it overnight. You can't force it by trying to push it through, because the jelly will go all cloudy when it's cooked. Won't do no good to your reputation down at the WI.

Next morning, measure a pound of sugar for every pint of liquid and put sugar and liquid in your cleaned-out jam-pan. Heat it gently to dissolve the sugar, then boil it for at least 10 to 15 minutes before testing it on a cold saucer to see if it's ready to set.

Pot it into clean hot jars like all the other jams and jellies.

Lemon Curd

About 6 good dollops of butter – ¾ lb
2lb bag of caster sugar
6 large lemons
8 eggs

Put the butter and sugar in a big bowl. Grate in the lemon peel and squeeze in the juice. Add the beaten eggs.

Put the bowl over a saucepan of water and cook on a medium heat, stirring a lot – watch out it doesn't turn into scrambled eggs – until it's thick. If you want to make it really smooth you can push it through a sieve.

Pour it into your hot jars, just like jam. It doesn't keep as long as jam, so make sure you eat it early on. Good for Christmas presents, anyway.

Apricot Jam

With most jams it is simply a matter of equal quantities of fruit and sugar, so they are all much of a muchness to make.

For about 10lb of apricot jam you'll need:

6lb apricots
1 pint of water
3 bags (6lb) of preserving sugar

Halve the apricots. If you want, you can crack a few of the stones, take out the nuts and add those to the fruit – they taste a bit like almonds.

Cook the fruit in the water until it's soft, then stir in the sugar and cook slowly until the sugar melts in. Bring it to the boil and keep it boiling well until it's ready. You must know by now how I test that – put some on a cold saucer, pop it in the fridge for a few seconds, then see if it wrinkles when you push it with your finger. You can tell when it's getting ready by sticking the wooden spoon in and letting the jam drop off – if it is starting to stick together and drop off in little lumps instead of in a stream, it's getting ready. Make sure you keep stirring so it doesn't stick.

Leave it to cool in the pan for a bit or else the fruit will all float to the top of the jars. Stir it to see if the fruit is staying well mixed into the mixture. And make sure your pots are good and warm when you put it in them. You don't want them cracking with the heat.

Put little waxed discs on straight away, then put the lids on when it's cool.

THE BEAU RIVAGE

Suppose it's typical of us, really – some people come back from their holidays in foreign parts with a packet of snapshots; we come back with a load of recipes. Well, you tell me a better way of remembering a holiday by the French seaside than having a bowl of mussels in white wine and garlic? The memory lingers on, as they say. So does the garlic. (We grow our own, now. Just brought some back and shoved the cloves in the ground.)

Those French know how to live, though. I thought it would be all snails and frog's legs. But they have some clever little dodges for making things taste good. I found myself getting out a pencil and paper and taking down recipes for the first time in my life. I missed not having potatoes with everything, though.

Not that they were letting us into any secrets when we first got there. Our first meal at the Hotel Beau Rivage made me think we'd have been better off booking a fortnight in Bexhill. It got better, though. Most things usually do, I find.

Moules Marinière

You need about 4lb of nice big mussels. In this country they seem to be better in the winter than the summer – not so many open and broken ones to throw away. In France they told me to leave them sitting in cold water for an hour to clean them out and get rid of the gritty bits. They even sprinkle a bit of flour on the water to help them clean themselves out.

You'll need:
A couple of shallots or small onions
A couple of cloves of garlic
A good dollop of butter – 2oz
A few sprigs of parsley and thyme
A big glass of white wine and a little less than that of water
Lemon juice and pepper
A good splash of fresh cream

You have to scrub the mussel shells really clean, scraping off as many of the little barnacles that cling to them as you can. You also have to pull off the hairy bit they call their beards. It all takes a bit of time, one of those bending-over-the-sink jobs. But worth it in the end.

Chop up the onion and garlic and fry them in the butter in a big pan until they're soft. Then add the herbs, wine and water and bring it up to the boil.

Turn down the heat, add the mussels and sprinkle them with plenty of pepper. They don't need salt. Put the lid on the pan, turn up the heat and shake it all around. In a few minutes all the mussel shells will have opened, showing their lovely orangey-yellow insides. (If there are any that won't open, chuck them out. They were dead to start with.)

Squeeze some lemon juice over them and spoon them into a great big bowl, leaving the liquid in the pan.

Add a good splash of cream to the pan and bubble it up to make a sauce. Taste it and add whatever it wants.

Pour the sauce over the mussels, add lots of chopped parsley and eat 'em with plenty of bread to mop up the sauce.

Châteaubriand

This is only their name for the thickest part of a fillet steak. But you have to watch out, because if you give them half a chance they'll just burn the outside under a grill or on some charcoal and leave the inside more or less raw. We like it underdone, but not uncooked. So Charlie taught us what to say – 'à point'. That's their way of saying 'medium', but once or twice we still had to send it back for a bit more under the grill.

Sometimes they roast it and serve it sliced up with a sauce of white wine, herbs and chopped shallots bubbled up in the pan juices. If I'm doing it that way I fry it in butter first to get it well browned on all sides and then pop it in a hot oven – 425°F/ 220°C/gas mark 7 – for between half and three-quarters of an hour, depending on how pink you want the inside.

The nice, thick juicy slices with the shallots sprinkled over them arranged across each other along a serving plate like a pack of cards look really good and French. If I'm grilling a piece, I just brush some melted butter on it and sprinkle salt and pepper on as I turn it. You'll know the technique already, for sure – nice and hot to start each side off so as to seal it and keep the juice in, then you can ease off the grill a bit to cook it through, turning it as often as you like.

Grilling time depends on the thickness, stands to reason. But one of the great, thick chunky bits they have could take as long as when I roast it. I do it by feel. The more solid and less sort of spongy it feels when you press it, the more it's cooked.

Potage du Jour

Couldn't get over how they used to plonk a whole big bowl of soup and a basket of bread on the table at the Beau Rivage, and leave us to help ourselves. Good cheap way of filling us up, though. In English it means 'Soup of the Day', which made me think every day would be different. Not on your Nellie! Nearly every day it was the same, made of left-over salad things like lettuce, spinach and that weed they grow in their gardens that we find under the hedge at home – sorrel.

Came to quite like it, though. And it's a good way of using up lettuces that have shot a bit.

About 1lb of salad leaves – anything you've got, like lettuce, watercress, spinach, sorrel. I suppose you could bung in some young nettles, too. Cleanses the blood, they say

A good knob of butter – 1-2oz
A couple of potatoes
A couple of pints of stock or more
Salt and pepper
An egg yolk
About half a teacup of cream – 3-4fl oz

Wash and chop the leaves and cook them in the butter in a big pan until they're soft – you could throw in a little chopped onion as well. Add the peeled and chopped potatoes and the stock and simmer it all until it's really soft – about half an hour.

At the Beau Rivage they just whirred it all up in something they called a Mouli Machine after that. But I like to make it smooth by pushing it through a sieve, so the softer you cook it the better. Then thicken it up with an egg yolk beaten with the cream, and salt and pepper to taste, and heat it up again gently.

Don't let it boil or it will curdle. If it's too thick, add some more stock.

Omelette au Fromage

Sounds better than a cheese omelette, doesn't it? But they had a way of turning them out light as a poet's pocket. They said the secret was their special pan with a thick bottom that they could heat up well so that the omelette cooked quickly. It's slow cooking that makes 'em tough.

For each one you need 4 fresh eggs, some salt and pepper and a handful of grated cheese in the middle just before you fold it over.

Melt a good dollop of butter in your omelette pan and heat it till it's foaming. Then pour in the eggs, which you've whisked up really well and seasoned with salt and pepper. They showed me how they give it a bit of a stir with a fork for a few seconds and then leave it alone. They leave their omlettes a bit runny in the middle, which seems to help make them lighter.

Sprinkle the cheese in the middle, fold the omelette in half and slide it onto a plate. The cheese will have melted into the runny bit in the middle.

You've got to eat it straight away, so I get everyone sat down and shove it at them out of the frying-pan. Don't suit Pop, though. Gives him heartburn.

Grilled Pork Chops with Haricots Verts

I couldn't work out what was different about their pork chops until I had a word with Alphonse, the chef. He used olive oil to brush the chops before cooking them. But it wasn't just plain oil. He kept it in jars with lots of other things floating in it – sprigs of herbs like thyme, crushed garlic, crushed peppercorns. It made all the difference, and yet they are the same as our chops.

So I brought back some olive oil and I've made up a jar of the mixture myself now. I cut the rind off some chops, brush them with the oil and give them about ten minutes on each side under the grill, until the fat is golden and crispy.

The 'Haricots Verts' are just those long, thin French beans given a few minutes in boiling water with the lid off, then tossed in butter with a few sliced spring onions.

Langoustines

Funny little things like baby lobsters. They used to serve them as starters on Thursdays, if the sea wasn't too rough. I've had them grilled with chips down on our coast, only they call 'em scampi. But the French just throw them in salted, boiling water for three minutes and eat them cold.

They are a bit of a fiddle and Pop used to tick on about them.

The only meat you can eat is in the tail, there's nothing in the claws. You won't get fat on them, but they taste good dipped in a bit of mayonnaise.

Fried Sardines

I got to like these in France, but you need half a dozen or so each. All I do is clean them and take the heads off, then dip them in some seasoned flour and cook them in butter like I do trout. By the time they are golden all over they'll be cooked inside. Nice snack, with a squeeze of lemon. And there's more to them than whitebait, I'll say that for them.

Saucisson à la Mode d'ici

According to Charlie, it means 'Bangers The Way We Do Them Here'. And a real surprise it was when it came. Nothing more than a giant sausage roll, made with puff pastry. Not a bad idea, I thought. So I do it often at home now.

You can do them any size you like and as fat or thin as you want, depending on how much sausage meat and pastry you have. I usually add some onion and herbs to the sausagemeat to give it a bit more flavour – about one onion and a tablespoon or two of herbs to each pound of sausagemeat.

Roll it up just like for sausage rolls. It has to be cooked in a high oven to get the pastry crisp and golden – say 400–425°F/200–220°C/gas mark 6-7 – for about three-quarters of an hour or more.

Pigeons à la Gautier

Named after a chap who was a poet, so it's nice and cheap and easy to make. The sauce of wine and cream goes well with the strong meat, too.

For every 4 pigeons you'll need:
8 rashers of streaky bacon
A knob of lard and a big knob of butter
A glass of white wine
About ½ pint of stock
About a teacup of fresh cream

Give the birds a good wipe inside and out then season them and wrap a couple of rashers of bacon round each one. You'll have to make a parcel of them with string.

Heat up the lard and butter in a big casserole dish that will go straight on top of the stove, then brown the birds well on all sides. Then drain away that fat. Pour the wine into the dish, let it bubble up, then pour in the stock and let the birds simmer with the lid on until they are tender.

Some of the pigeons we get are tough old birds. I tell 'em, why don't you shoot younger ones? A young one will be ready after an hour of simmering. An older one takes much longer. You can stick a skewer into the fat part of the leg to test. They want to be really tender.

Take them out and untie them when they are done, and make the sauce with the juices in the bottom of the pan. First – a trick Alphonse at the hotel taught me – you mix some soft butter and flour into a knob (about a tablespoon of each), then throw it in the pan and whisk it up until it thickens in the heat. If it seems too thick, add some more wine or stock; more butter and flour if it's too thin. Play around with it until it seems right, add whatever salt and pepper you think, then stir in the cream.

You can pour this over the birds or serve it separate in a jug. Turns a pigeon into a poem.

Hare with Burgundy and Prunes

A fellow called Old Netty brings us hares in a sack sometimes. We used to plain jug them, but we prefer this way since we tasted it in France. The prunes sweeten up the rich meat a treat.

1 hare, cleaned and chopped into about 12 pieces
Butter and lard for frying
A good lump of bacon – about ½ lb cut into little pieces
2 onions, chopped
1 heaped serving-spoon of plain flour – 3oz
A bottle of Burgundy wine
About a pint of stock
A clove or two of garlic
A bay leaf
A couple of dozen baby onions
A couple of dozen prunes
A couple of dozen little mushrooms

You need a big pan to brown up the bits of hare all over in the butter and lard. Put them in a big casserole that will go on top of the stove, then fry up the bacon and chopped onion and add that to the hare.

Pour off all but a couple of spoonfuls of fat from the frying-pan, then stir in the flour and cook it a bit until it's browned. Then stir in the wine and the stock (I told you that you needed a nice big pan) and bring it to the boil.

Pour it over the hare and then add the garlic, the bay leaf and some salt and pepper – depending on how salty your bacon is. Add the onions, prunes and mushrooms and simmer it for at least an hour, until the hare is tender.

You have to keep check every now and then to make sure it's not sticking on the bottom and give it a good stir.

To my mind it's got an even better flavour the next day, after it's been left and re-heated.

Party Menu

We had a bit of a do in the Beau Rivage to celebrate Mariette and Charlie's first anniversary. We worked out the menu with Alphonse the chef, so it's French with a touch of good old England as well . . .

Charentais Melon au Porto

I don't know why all that pressing and poking of melons goes on when people want to see if they are ripe. All you have to do is smell 'em. If it smells sweet, it's ripe. Charentais are the green and white striped ones with the pretty orange middles. Slice them in half, take out the seeds and take a little slice off the bottom of each one so they stand up. Then I dollop in a good splash of Pop's port.

Filets de Sole aux Truffes

Personally I think it's hard to beat a nice, fresh grilled Dover sole with nothing on it but some butter and lemon juice. But this is very tasty for when you want something a bit more special.

8 nice fillets of sole
A couple of shallots
A few sprigs of parsley and a bay leaf
A small glass of white wine and about half as much of water
A dollop of butter – about 2oz

A serving-spoon of plain flour – about 1oz
2 egg yolks
¼ pint of fresh cream
Parsley and some chopped truffles (if you can get 'em, though you'll probably have to take your shopping bag to France)

Fold the fish fillets in half, or roll them up if you like, and put them in a dish that will go in the oven. Sprinkle the shallots and herbs on top, then pour in the wine and water and give them a shake of salt and pepper.

Cover with a greaseproof paper and pop them in a low oven – about 325°F/170°C/gas mark 3 – for 10-15 minutes, until just cooked. Keep the fish warm while you're making the sauce. You need to get all the liquid out of the dish and sieve it, because that gives the sauce its taste.

Melt half the butter in a pan and stir in the flour, cooking it very gently over a low heat so that it doesn't go at all brown. Then stir in all the fishy liquid, and keep on stirring it until it gets hot.

Mix up the egg yolks and cream and stir them into the sauce – but you've got to be dead cunning about making sure it's not too hot, otherwise it'll curdle. Just warm it through nicely.

Give it a taste, and add some salt, pepper or lemon juice if you think it could do with it. This is where you stir in your chopped truffle if you've got it and some parsley. Then pour it over your dish of fish. I usually sprinkle a bit of truffle and parsley over it. A few prawns on top makes it look like what they serve up in London at a quid a go!

Rost Bif with Yorkshire Pudding

You can't get more English than that, so we had a little chat with Alphonse to make sure he knew what he was doing. Didn't want it raw.

We had a sirloin, which they called *contre filet* or something. I like a rib or sirloin on the bone best of all, as long as it's got a nice marbling of fat in the lean to give it that perfect beefy flavour.

Each rib weighs about 2lb, and I don't usually get less than four. So the butcher ends up giving me an 8-10lb joint. That takes 3-4 hours to cook on quite a high oven, say 425°F/220°C/gas mark 7. At least I have it at that heat to start it off, and make sure it's the same heat at the end, when the Yorkshire and roast potatoes are in. But in the middle I often have it right down to medium hot – about 350°F/180°C/gas mark 4.

There's nothing much to roasting the meat, I just give it a wipe and put it fat-side up in my big roasting tin. I sprinkle it with salt and pepper and rub in a bit of dry mustard as well.

Keep basting it when it's in the oven to get the fat crispy. You can see how the meat is getting on by testing it with a skewer. Pink juices means it's pink in the middle, and the clearer they get the more well done it'll be.

While the meat is cooking I mix the batter for the Yorkshire pudding. I take a bit of pride in my technique for this.

You need:
6 heaped serving-spoons of plain flour – ½ lb
Pinch of salt
2 eggs
Half a pint of milk
Half a pint of water

Sieve the flour and salt into a bowl, make a hole in the centre, drop in the eggs and half the liquid, mixing it to a nice smooth batter. If you put the eggs and the milk in the hole in the middle, you can gradually draw in the flour from the sides as you mix, using a wooden spoon.

When it's all mixed up, you have to carry on beating to get it smooth. I use the back of the spoon and plenty of wristy slapping. The more the better, several minutes if you are really keen. When you've got plenty of bubbles floating on it, you can stir in the rest of the milk and water to make it like thin cream.

To cook it, pour off some of the fat from around the meat into a big baking-tin – the one I've got is about 12x15 inches and it'll take about two-thirds of the batter. The rest goes into my trays of individual pudding tins. You should be able to make up to another six in them, not forgetting to put a spot of dripping in the bottom before putting them in the oven.

You want to get the tins really hot before putting in the batter. Then give the small ones about half an hour and the big one about three-quarters of an hour in the hot oven, until they are golden and puffed up. It should come up light as a butterfly.

All you need then is the gravy. Stir some flour into the meat juices after you've taken the joint out to rest a bit before carving. Cook and stir until it's thickened, then add some water from the vegetables and cook it to a nice thick gravy.

Crêpes Suzettes

Posh for pancakes.
For the batter:
A couple of heaped serving-spoons of plain flour – 3oz
Pinch of salt
1 heaped serving-spoon of caster sugar
1 egg and 1 extra yolk
About a third of a pint of milk
Melted butter

For the filling:
2 good dollops of soft butter – ¼ lb
4 heaped serving-spoons of caster sugar – ¼ lb
Grated rind and juice of one orange
1 tablespoon of orange liqueur and 4 tablespoons of brandy – raid the cocktail cabinet

Milk up the flour, salt, sugar, eggs and milk as you would an ordinary batter for Yorkshire pudding. Then add a couple of tablespoons of melted butter.

This'll make about 12 nice thin pancakes. Fry them in a pan with plenty of butter to make them golden, tossing them over half way through.

Mix up the butter, sugar, orange rind and juice with the orange liqueur, and when the pancakes are cool dollop a bit in the middle of each one, before folding them up into a triangle.
Pop the rest of the butter in a big frying-pan and lay the pancakes out on top.

This is the showy bit. If you've got a spirit lamp you can do it at the table. Warm the pan full of pancakes and butter slowly on top of the stove. When the butter is all melted and sizzling, slosh in the brandy and bubble it up a bit more. Then get a match and set fire to it. Dish 'em out while they're hot and juicy.

At the Beau Rivage, they always liked to serve their Brie and fruit before pudding – funny lot.

CHARLIE'S NOTES